P9-CCW-818

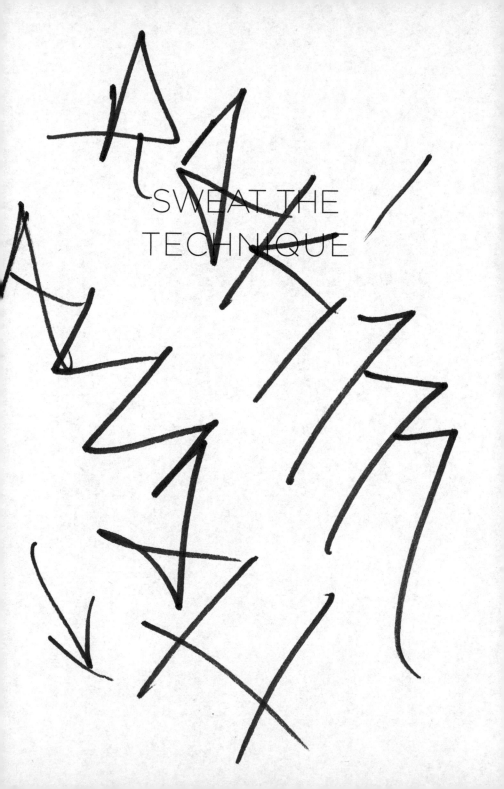

SWEAT THE
TECHNIQUE

SWEAT THE TECHNIQUE

REVELATIONS ON CREATIVITY
FROM THE LYRICAL GENIUS

RAKIM

WITH **BAKARI KITWANA**

Amistad

An Imprint of HarperCollinsPublishers

The names and identifying characteristics of certain individuals have been changed to protect their privacy.

"Eric B. Is President," "My Melody," and "Move the Crowd," lyrics and music by Eric Barrier and William Griffin. Copyright © 1987, Universal Songs of PolyGram International, Inc., on behalf of itself and Robert Hill Music.

"Flow Forever," lyrics and music by William Griffin, Robert Davis, and Antonio Franklin. Copyright © 1999 Sony/ATV Music Publishing.

"Follow the Leader" and "Lyrics of Fury," lyrics and music by Eric Barrier and William Griffin. Copyright © 1988 Sony/ATV Music Publishing.

"Mahogany," lyrics and music by Eric Barrier and William Griffin. Copyright © 1990 Sony/ATV Music Publishing.

"The Mystery: Who is God," lyrics and music by William Griffin, Dan Fisher, Ervin Drake, and Irene Higgenbothem. Copyright © 1997 Sony/ATV Music Publishing.

"18th Letter Always and Forever," lyrics and music by William Griffin and Scott Phillips. Copyright © 1997 Sony/ATV Music Publishing.

"Musical Massacre," lyrics and music by William Griffin, Eric Barrier, James Castor, John Pruitt, and Gerry Thomas. Copyright © 1988 Sony/ATV Music Publishing.

All lyrics used by permission. All rights reserved.

SWEAT THE TECHNIQUE. Copyright © 2019 by Rakim & Associates, Inc. All rights reserved. Printed in the United States of America. No part of this book may be used or reproduced in any manner whatsoever without written permission except in the case of brief quotations embodied in critical articles and reviews. For information, address HarperCollins Publishers, 195 Broadway, New York, NY 10007.

HarperCollins books may be purchased for educational, business, or sales promotional use. For information, please email the Special Markets Department at SPsales@harpercollins.com.

FIRST EDITION

Designed by SBI Book Arts, LLC

Library of Congress Cataloging-in-Publication Data has been applied for.

ISBN 978-0-06-285023-2

19 20 21 22 23   LSC   10 9 8 7 6 5 4 3 2 1

For the Creators:
Whatever your medium, whatever your message,
I've written this book for you.

CONTENTS

PART TWO
INSPIRATION

PART THREE
SPIRITUALITY

PART FOUR
CONSCIOUSNESS

PART FIVE
ENERGY

OUTRO

PROLOGUE

As the hour approaches, I gather my thoughts and escape to a room with the bare necessities. I transform. I enter the zone.

I focus

I stare at blank walls until they become movie screens giving me a front-row seat to the world.

I focus

Until the Earth's high pitch sound multiplies in my ears only muffled by my thoughts. My mind superseding body I force my life to flash before my eyes again and again. Before I know it, I'm somewhere between conscious and subconscious. My universal awareness heightens.

I focus

Seeing vicariously through everyone's eyes. I can astral project to any place, any time. Past, present, and future. Imagination challenges my reality. Creative juices start to take over. Try to tap into that divine universal source of knowledge until my art speaks as many languages as possible. Try to broaden my horizons and in return achieve omnipresence.

I focus

Then finally it hits me. The original idea.

I'm focused.

SWEAT THE TECHNIQUE

THE DOOR

I hear the same questions all the time. What's it mean to be a writer? A rapper? A lyricist? Where do I go in my mind to create the perfect rhyme? What energy do I channel to move an audience? To manipulate syllables into syncopated flow and paint a story with words and music? How do I get someone to stop a record, rewind, replay, and rethink everything they thought they heard the first time?

What made me sit down thirty years ago and say, "My name is Rakim Allah, and I'm about to flip the whole script"?

My writing starts in an empty room. It doesn't really matter where because I have written everywhere. It's just me and Four White Walls. Maybe one that just has some paint peeling in a corner of the ceiling or maybe one that has a window that looks out over the lights of a great city with those million stories bouncing through the streets. It can be a studio, a hotel, or the back of a bus. Probably they aren't even white, but when I sit down, in my mind, it's four walls that are as blank as the notebook I'm staring down at.

It has to start with dead silence. I have to turn off that morning's music and distance myself from the distractions of life's cacophony. No phones, no kids, no entourage or onlookers. I need to completely tune out so I can start to tune in.

I focus on my purpose. That's what has brought me into this room and that's what will guide me now that I'm here. I dig back into the bag of observations and experiences that inspire me and start to craft a storyline. I inject the spirituality that gives so much of that inspiration a greater sense of place and remember that my Self, my listeners, and my culture expect and deserve more than simplicity. They deserve a conscious message delivered through a thoughtful collection of ideas that are more than the words on the page.

And that's when I start to hear it.

Just a pitch or a tone . . . a buzzing energy emanating from origins beyond each of us individually but encompassing all of us universally. The energy takes a frequency, and the frequency forms into an idea. That idea takes inspiration from everything I've learned and observed, and blends it with awareness of my self and my artistry. And it breaks the silence with music that's blended with memories and molded into something original.

My pen starts to flow. The lines in my notebook fill up and spill over to paint pictures on the white walls around me. The rhymes come from anywhere. They come from everywhere. I might have a story in mind that unfolds step by step or I might just know the end and have to work my way back. I could start with one bar or one phrase or even one word and circle around that, guided by the frequency, until the track takes full form. I draw from my knowledge and add the tricks of my technique to slip in messages that range from subtle to unavoidable. I wrap around wordplay and push boundaries of form.

I stay focused on my intentions. Make something original. Outdo what I've already done. Write something to force the conscious listener to think, the music lover to clap, and every other rapper to turn their head and say, "Damn." I want to build monuments of monologue that stand the test of time.

To guide artists and non-creatives alike through these revelations, I've channeled my reflections into 5 Pillars of Creativity: Purpose, Inspiration, Spirituality, Consciousness, and Energy.

This is who I am and this is how I do it.

ORIGINS

I was born in Wyandanch, New York, about an hour outside of New York City in Suffolk County, Long Island. At four and a half square miles with around eleven thousand residents at any given time, Wyandanch isn't even a town. It's a hamlet, one of seven that make up the larger town of Babylon, but if you lived in Wyandanch, that's what you identified with. Wyandanch didn't have a bunch of big buildings; it didn't have any projects. It was pretty much a bunch of single-family houses built in the 1950s, studded with fruit trees in people's perfectly manicured yards branching out from Wyandanch Park, Carver Park (named after George Washington Carver), and Lincoln Park. The main strip was called Straight Path, and it was filled with your typical barbershops, tailors, hardware stores, and food spots. At night, that's where the little social clubs and bars would light up, and it's where the dealers and the hustlers would come out of the shadows.

My neighborhood wasn't rich, but it never felt poor. And it was predominantly Black. In the '40s and '50s, Long Island had a lot of communities—Levittown, about twelve miles west, being the most historically famous—that didn't allow ownership by Black families. The developers would prohibit "non-white occupants" right in their contracts, so when a real estate agent would advertise a community as interracial, that's where the Blacks would buy . . . and only the Blacks. Wyandanch definitely had a working-class community, but because of that openness in a sea of segregation, you also had lawyers, doctors, businesspeople, teachers, and all sorts of professionals with dreams of financial independence. In a place like that, everyone knows almost everyone, and if you don't know them directly, you know their brother or their sister or their cousin. It's one of those places where a kid can get raised by the village. And it's where my parents settled and decided to start their family.

A few years earlier, Cynthia Harewood saw a man across the room in a nightclub and told her girlfriends she was going to marry him before she even knew his name. Willie Griffin, his legal name, fell in love with her as well, and they would go on to spend over thirty years together as husband and wife and mother and father. I was the youngest of their five children, after Ronald, Robyn, Steven, and Stephanie, but people always called me an old soul. Maybe that was because I was always running around going to parties with my older brothers and sisters . . . maybe it was the whiskers I developed a lot younger than most. Maybe, and I'm not proud of this, it was getting my first gun charge at age twelve or, and this I am proud of, not backing down from anyone who would challenge me or my family down on the strip that I was definitely too young to be hanging on.

But I like to think my tendency toward maturity was a little more destined. I was conceived during the urban riots of the Long Hot Summer of 1967 and born on January 28, 1968, three months before the assassination of Dr. Martin Luther King Jr. My mother heard—and, by extension, I believe I heard—the words of Dr. King while I was still in the womb, and that sparked a connection to the man that resonates with me still. My parents thought about naming me Willie, after my father, so I was almost a junior. At the last minute my father said no. "I don't want him to be a junior. I want him to be his own man."

"Well, then, name him William," Mom said. So for a short while I was William Michael Griffin, but one day I was crying in my grandmother's arms when she said, "Poppo, stop crying."

"That's cute," Mom said. The name stuck. Soon Poppo became Pop, and growing up, everyone called me Pop. People outside the family didn't even know my given name.

At our house whenever an aunt or an uncle or a friend walked in, my father told us to perform. If they came by late and we were all asleep, my father woke us up to sing and dance in our pajamas. We were a musical family—my brothers and sisters knew how to sing, play piano, and play the sax, so we were like our own band, but I always liked to break out with a little solo. Sometimes I played Michael Jackson and would line my brothers and sisters up behind me like the Jackson 5. I used to practice in the bathroom mirror and sing "Dancing Machine" over and over while watching myself, making sure my movements were just like his when he did it. When company came over, I did my little routine with all his moves and hitting all his notes. Whatever character I played, it always brought the house down, and I came to love the feeling of electrifying a crowd. I wanted it all the time. I couldn't wait for people to come over and let me show them my skills, because having everyone watch me just felt right.

I was six the first time I saw hip-hop. It was the summer of

1974. My big brother Stevie took me to see it. They didn't call it hip-hop or rap back then, but it was already a lot more than just a sound. It was a whole experience. Late at night, in Wyandanch Park, they had a DJ with a big sound system that was plugged into a street lamppost and B-boys dancing and guys on the mic spitting little rhymes. These guys were the early rappers, and these parties were the beginning of hip-hop. The parties were happening in the Bronx, Queens, Brooklyn, uptown—all over New York. DJs were taking disco, soul, and funk records—anything that was high-energy and powerful and danceable—and isolating the breakdown, the part where it's just rhythm, percussion, and drumming that makes people want to dance with some force. Any record could become part of a rap DJ's set because DJs weren't concerned with the whole record. They focused on those breaks and mixed two copies of the record back and forth so they could extend the break and change the power of the record entirely.

Everyone learned the sonic power of the break from DJ Kool Herc, a Jamaican immigrant from the South Bronx who started spinning parties in the rec room of the building where he lived. In August of 1973 his sister Cindy wanted money to buy clothes for school, so she told Herc to throw a party and charge admission. Down in that rec room he became one of the fathers of rap. He had a big system with Godzilla-sized Shure speakers, so his music was loud. He spun on the breaks and sometimes he got on the mic and said little rhythmic phrases into an echo chamber. Stuff like "Kool Herc! Go to work! Go to work!" Simple stuff. "Y'all feeling all right?! To the beat, y'all! B-boys, are you ready? B-girls, are you ready?" He said "B" for "break," for the dancers who'd go off on the breaks. They weren't rhymes. They were like the zygotes that were the beginnings of the monster that would become MC'ing.

Herc spun parties all around the New York City metropolitan area, including on Long Island at Wyandanch Park. I was really young, but I was there, and I can still see his gigantic speakers that looked like fifty-five-gallon garbage cans. They were so loud they shook the ground like the music was creating an earthquake. Herc went all around the city, spreading the gospel of hip-hop. His formula was to extend the breakdown part so the serious dancers could get down and perform for the crowd. It wasn't music meant to get boys and girls dancing together. It was music meant to get boys dancing instead of fighting in gangs. New York had a gang issue before early rap came along, and it mostly ended when the gangsters transitioned into music. A lot of early dancing was about warring crews battling by break-dancing without ever touching each other. Symbolic violence was a lot better than killing. But the new culture scared most club owners, so Herc and the other pioneering hip-hop DJs were playing for people who loved the music and would follow it anywhere. They went into the parks, and at those parties they started building a culture.

It quickly became a way of life for a lot of people in the hood in late-1970s New York City. The culture stretched beyond the music and included break-dancing or B-boying and graffiti art, and you could dress hip-hop with a Kangol hat and Adidas shell toes or Puma Clydes. I always believed there was a hip-hop way of thinking, because listening to this music was like taking musical steroids. It was sonic confidence. It made you bop harder, stand up straighter, stick your chest out more. It fed your ego. At a time when a lot of people in the hood were getting strangled by poverty, hip-hop came along and offered a boost of confidence and a jolt of fun. It was music from the hood for the hood, meant to make people feel good. And it spread like wildfire. In my elementary school years, everyone I knew around my age loved hip-hop. It was almost like the shared religion of our tribe. I loved every aspect of the culture and tried my hand at all of it. When I wasn't trying to DJ, I would pop-lock with my friends for hours, then go get the canvases out and do some graffiti, then get with some rappers and kick freestyles. As soon as I knew what rap was, I was in love.

Once, Maniack, a local DJ who was friends with my brother Stevie, brought his equipment to our house. I was so young I wasn't really tall enough to reach the turntables. Stevie and him sat there drinking beers and spinning records while I watched every little thing they did. I microscoped the whole situation. Stevie and Maniack decided to run out to get more beer, but first they took the needles off and hid them. They were hiding them from me, but I knew where they put them. As soon as I heard the front door close, I went over to the shelf, reached behind the picture frame, and grabbed the needles. I pulled out two milk crates and stood up on them to screw on the needles, and I got some records going and started trying to cut back and forth between them, but somehow I hit the pitch control knob so one of the records started going really fast, and I didn't know how to change it. I panicked a little because the sound was going crazy. Before I came up with a solution, my brother and Maniack walked into the room and looked at me like *What the hell is going on?*

"Boy, get off them turntables! Stop playing around!" Stevie yelled.

"Nah, man, let him finish," Maniack said, more curious than angry. "I wanna see what he does."

He showed me how to change the pitch so the record played at the right speed, then I was able to chill out and start mixing.

I was so good they were shocked at how much I'd picked up just from watching them.

I was seven when I wrote my first rhyme. I had seen guys on the block rhyming and wanted to try it. I wrote, "Mickey Mouse built a house / he built it by the border / an earthquake came and rocked his crib / and now it's in the water." Now I had the DJ'ing bug. With some life experience and some work on my vocabulary, I could start bringing things together.

FROM THE PARKS
TO THE STUDIO

I began my senior year of high school thinking my next move was going to Stony Brook University to play quarterback. The head coach said it was possible I could start freshman year. I planned to go to college and focus on football, not rapping. At DJ Maniack's house, I'd made a beat and rhymed over it for sixty minutes, filling up both sides of a Memorex tape. My plan was to play that tape when I got to college to let everyone know who I was as an MC. I wasn't gonna battle everyone there. I'd just play my tape so they'd all know who was the best MC on campus, so I could shut the whole conversation down and get back to football.

A few days after I made that tape, my homeboy Alvin Toney knocked on my door with some tall guy I didn't know hovering behind him. Alvin was my dude, but I used to tell my friends, if you come by my crib, come by yourself and definitely don't bring nobody I don't know.

I opened the door and gave Alvin a look that could kill, which kindly might be interpreted as *What do you think you doin'?*

"Yo, come outside for a minute," he said, sensing he had violated my trust.

"I got my shorts on, man," I said hesitantly.

"This guy knows Marley Marl and Mr. Magic," Alvin said. "He wants to make a record. His name is Eric." Those were two of the biggest names in hip-hop at that moment. Marley was the hottest producer in the game, and he was really shaping the sound of hip-hop with the records he produced for MC Shan and Roxanne Shante. Mr. Magic was a powerful radio DJ on WBLS who was then one of the few jocks playing rap records on the radio. Someone who knew both of them had to be for real.

I said, "He can come in."

That's how I met Eric B.

He was working in promotions at WBLS. He'd drive around the New York tristate area in a WBLS van and DJ parties in the community to help spread the name of the radio station—what they now call a street team. This took him all over, but he was in Wyandanch a lot so he had a lot of friends there. He was thinking about making a DJ album, presenting a group of MCs, like all the best MCs he'd met traveling around for his job. So he was asking people in every town, "Who's the nicest MC around?" When he asked that in Wyandanch, of course he ended up at my place.

I put on the tape I'd made for Stony Brook, and after five minutes Eric said, "Yo, we can go to Marley Marl's crib and make a record right now."

I said, "That's cool, but I can't sign a contract."

"Why?"

"I'm going to college to play football. If I sign a deal, I'll be ineligible to play."

"We can do it where you're the guest on the record. If it's

my record and you're the special guest, you don't have to sign a contract."

I was down with any plan that wouldn't kill my football eligibility.

About a week later Eric and I took the train from Long Island to Queensbridge, forty-five minutes, to go to Marley Marl's studio, where so many hot records had been made with artists like MC Shan, Roxanne Shante, and Biz Markie to name a few. We were going to the place where hip-hop was being built, the most important studio in the game.

Marley's "studio" was actually his sister's apartment on the second floor of Queensbridge Houses, the now legendary housing project in Long Island City, Queens, that over the years was home to MC Shan, Marley Marl, Nas, and others. Marley had taken it over. I walked past the kitchen and into the living room to find the mixing boards, the keyboards, the speakers, the drum machine, tons of vinyl records—everything you need to record, with a microphone set up on a stand where the coffee table should be. We sat on the couch and started vibing about music and records and what we wanted to do in the session. I had my Stony Brook tape, so Marley took that and started adding his special touches to one of the beats. When he was done, he handed me the mic and said it was time for me to start laying down the verses. I used rhymes from the tape for Stony Brook, which I'd actually written a year before, and we called it "My Melody." Sitting on the couch in that living room just felt right. I was relaxed, and my flow was coming through smooth just like I wanted.

Marley said, "Yo, that was dope! Let's do it again with a little more energy."

Years before that moment, back when I was rhyming in the

park, I would rhyme all amped up because that got me heard in that loud outdoor environment. Plus, that was the way most people did it in the early days. That was the style of Run-DMC and LL Cool J. They kinda shouted on the mic as if they were giving a pep talk to a football team before the Super Bowl. It sounded forceful and tough. I respected those MCs, but I didn't want to sound like that. I wanted to be more thought-provoking, and if people were going to really hear my ideas and the intricacies of my rhymes, it was better to have a calmer delivery. I had to yell in the park, but when I went into the basement studios, I saw that I could rhyme without yelling. I liked being more conversational because then I could have more control over the tones in my voice, and you'd be better able to really hear me. If you could hear me, then you'd have to think about what I was saying. I put a good deal of effort into intentionally changing my delivery, and over time I taught myself how to remain calm while I rhymed. With that, I sounded like no one else—and I loved that. So when Marley asked me to do it with more energy, he didn't know that he was side stepping into a journey I'd been on for a while. I knew the sort of MC I wanted to be, and I wasn't going to let anyone, not even the great Marley Marl, change me.

Still on the couch, I started again. I laid the verse down in the same calm way I had the first time.

"I like the lines, but try to put more energy into it." After the fourth take, he said, "Maybe if you stand up it'll have a little more energy."

He was starting to annoy me. I said, "Yo, I could stand, I could sit, it don't matter. It's gonna sound the same."

An hour later we were still at an impasse. Marley kept whispering to Eric B. that I was rhyming too slow and it was giving him a headache. He didn't get why this young kid wasn't listening to a seasoned veteran. "I did Shante, I did Shan, I know what an MC's supposed to sound like," Marley finally yelled out, clearly at the end of his patience.

"Marley, it's a new day," Eric replied, not mad at all with the situation, his words hanging in the air.

Then MC Shan showed up and went into the kitchen with Marley. Shan was the pride of Queens, one of the first MCs to get signed to a major label, but they didn't know how to market him, so he eventually got dropped.

Marley left and Shan came back in and said, "Yo, Marley had to step out for a minute. He went to the store, so I'm going to produce the session." We started recording again, and Shan was blown away by my first take. "Oh my God!" he yelled. "This kid is ice-cold! I write lyrics. I know what's up. He's amazing!" Then he said, "That was great, but, yo Lord, why don't you put a little more energy in it?"

Here we go again, I thought.

Shan said, "Marley knows what he's talking about. A little more energy won't hurt you."

"This is how I roll," I told Shan, unwilling to budge.

Marley came back, and we finished "My Melody," but he was frustrated. "He don't take instructions, he don't listen to no one. His rhymes are great, but he's gonna put people to sleep."

On the Long Island Railroad train back to Wyandanch, I couldn't help but wonder if Marley was right about my style and if I should maybe have taken the direction he was giving. He was the professional. A producer with a string of big tracks and rappers with record deals banging on his apartment door. I was a kid with a mix tape I was going to use to impress other MCs on a college campus. I struggled with it for what seemed like the longest train ride I'd ever taken, but in the end, I knew that my laid-back style was what I needed. I'm calm most of the time in life, so that's how I rhyme. If I gave in easily and tried to be something I'm not, neither the success nor the failure that might come would be my own. I decided I'd made the right choice and nothing before or after was going to stop me being me.

Eric and I got back to the house and headed straight for the basement. That was the entertainment zone, and Moms had it hooked up. She was always hosting family and friends down there, so the place was stacked with vinyl of all genres and eras, records everywhere, and posters and album covers. It had a vibe. We looked through Mom's vinyl, and I pulled out James Brown's "Funky President." Eric pulled out Fonda Rae's "Over Like a Fat Rat." I was drinking a strawberry wine cooler—I really liked them back then—but when E. pulled out that record, I spat it out all over the wall and burst out laughing. I said, "Fonda Rae will never mix with James Brown!"

I started writing a new song in the basement of my parents' house, sitting on a stool by the bar, feeling euphoric. I was like, *World, here I come*. I just knew a lot of people would hear this one—more than a bunch of people in the park. Thousands! That feeling shaped the song. I wanted to make something that let people know who I was. The first thing I wrote was "I came in the door, I said it before, I never let the mic magnetize me no more." I said "never let the mic magnetize me no more" to emphasize this: Although the mic used to have control over me, now I have control over it. It used to draw me in like a magnet, but now I'm a real MC, and in my relationship with the mic, I'm in control.

I finished the song in a couple of hours.

The next night we went back to Marley's. I was amazed by Marley's ability to bring my James Brown beat and Eric's Fonda Rae beat together perfectly. He played the bass line on the synthesizer, and I got on the mic. "I came in the door . . ." This time Marley didn't complain about my energy. He just let me go. Maybe I was giving it a little more pep, but I got the feeling that Marley was starting to see what I was doing.

Eric named it "Eric B. Is President" even though I never said that phrase in the song. He did that partly because the sample was from "Funky President" and partly because Eric wanted to build his reputation as a famous DJ. Also, it was a time in hip-hop when, among the underground fan base, the DJs still enjoyed a degree of celebrity that nearly paralleled MCs. I thought the title was a little corny, but I've always loved what we did with that record.

PURPOSE

How to Emcee

[Hook]

It don't matter if I ain't on the page you on.
Tell me what you want, I give it to you the way you want,
show you how to flow and how to rip any phrase you want.
You just keep your eye on me, I show you how to emcee.
If it's wack ordinary displays you want,
tell what you want, I give it to you the way you want,
show you how to flow and how to rip any stage you on.
I can show you how to emcee like I got a degree.
This is your Qur'an or Bible
To be a true emcee icon or idol.
The contents you put in your songs are vital.
Like training for the UFC you want a title.
Slam thoughts on a canvas, flip 'em and pin 'em, metaphors
*   and similes and synonyms in 'em*
Spit heat around the town the more you get it heard till you spit
*   at two thousand miles before it hit a curve*

Then flaunt your rhymes and your rap pages wordplay to punch
   lines and catch phrases
Deep spots with players and ballers new game street talk
   straight off the corners new slang
I got heat for crowds for those that pursuit it
Spitters I show you flow till your vocals are fluid
From social to freestyle just focus into it
If you a G I'll show you how the Coppola do it.

[Hook]

Forever sick like catching AIDS is
In a class of greatness for magic phrases
My predicates last for pages
every letter fit trend setter like fashion statements
When folks get a sign and a hope forever
I wrote some of the illest rhymes ever put together
Soon as I make 'em rappers take 'em
analyze 'em for days and paraphrase 'em
I'm back hip-hoppers'll back my scripts and documents
Raps hit the block it's a wrap it's the apocalypse
The hood give my rap flow names
like 9/11 and crack cocaine.
I hit the building, it gets hotter in 'em.
It's like birds, most rappers don't know how to flip 'em.
Gotta hip 'em, get hop and show 'em how to spit 'em
I bus a rhyme and I school 'em for free, I scholarship 'em.

[Song]

Competition know the deal, you're not ready now.
Because you're dealing with the R, know how it's going down.

This is it if you so sick where your skills at? No sir, ghostwriter,
   you can kill that.
It's hard, this intricate flippin' it,
it isn't bars, it's infinite. So Ra deliverin' it far different.
Part lyricist, part instrument.
Start spittin' the articulate ya'll rhythms get
till every syllable you drop is pivotal.
If it's not original, it's not as memorable.
Ill lyrical till you so popular they sick of you
Pandemical threat level five it's critical
Kill 'em off with a word like euthanasia
till it spread to the youth in Asia.
In the booth I'm major,
my music's monumental, I'm a mogul.
You gonna make sense, I'ma show you.
You got to put yo life in them lines,
make it def hear sight to the blind,
make your flow tighter, brighter design,
so if the mic is your grind then biting's a crime,
especially if a ghostwriter's writin' your rhymes.

[Hook]

It don't matter if I ain't on the page you on.
Tell me what you want, I give it to you the way you want,
show you how to flow and how to rip any phrase you want,
you just keep your eye on me, I show you how to emcee.
If it's wack ordinary displays you want,
tell what you want, I give it to you the way you want,
show you how to flow and how to rip any stage you on.
I can show you how to emcee like I got a degree.

Notes on "How to Emcee"

Months after we made "My Melody" and "Eric B. Is President"
at Marley Marl's studio, we went into Power Play Studios
in Queens to record the rest of our first album, including
"I Ain't No Joke." I wanted us to sample the James Brown
Band's horns on "Pass the Peas," but Eric said he wanted to
scratch it. At first I was hesitant to try it that way. But when
we started doing it, I liked the way it sounded because it gave
the track that real hip-hop feeling. That took me right back to
the park and basement functions where I first started getting
on the mic. Now I was able to rhyme like I used to rhyme,
which made "I Ain't No Joke" one of my favorite joints on
that album.

"How to Emcee" is almost like "I Ain't No Joke 2.0." There's
so much working in that song: braggadocio, metaphors,
wordplay. It's one of them joints where I was letting myself
have a little fun. By the time "How to Emcee" was released on
The Seventh Seal album in 2009, the message was similar to
my goal with "I Ain't No Joke": "I'm so dope on the mic that
you cats need to be checking in on this, and as a matter of
fact, I could show *you* how to be no joke on the mic." It's just
an "I'm that dude" type of song—a How to Emcee 101 course
for other rappers in a song that says, "If you want to learn
how to rhyme, just follow me."

Partly an evolution from "I Ain't No Joke" (which in 1987
said, "Hey, I know what I'm doing") and "Don't Sweat the
Technique" (which in 1992 called out fellow rappers trying
to copy what I was doing), "How to Emcee" in 2009 said "All

right, if you're trying to copy me, you are obviously doing it wrong, so I'll show you what I'm doing." Additionally, "How to Emcee" was a commentary on the dumbed-down rap scene at the time. So few artists in 2009 were using real skills or anything that made you think. I felt it was a perfect time to say, "Yeah, I'll teach y'all how to rap." That was my sarcastic flow.

Also, in this song there's a lot of what I call wordplay. For example, when I say, "I'm back. Hip-hoppers'll back my scripts and documents. / Rap hit the block, it's a wrap, it's the apocalypse," I use two words twice ("back" and "rap"/"wrap"), but with different meanings. When I say, "Kill 'em off with a word like euthanasia / till it spread to the youth in Asia," it's more wordplay, having a little fun. But then I tell them how to mix words: "It's hard, this intricate flippin' it, / it isn't bars, it's infinite. So Ra deliverin' it far different. / Part lyricist, part instrument. / Start spittin' the more articulate y'all rhythms get / till every syllable you drop is pivotal. / If it's not original, it's not memorable." I'm having fun with the syllables. I'm also providing lessons in rhyming, so if you listen to it, you can get something from it: "make your flow tighter, brighter design, / so if the mic is your grind, then biting's a crime, / especially if a ghostwriter's writin' your rhymes."

This song is also the closest to a structured song that I ever used because it has the hook-verse, hook-verse consistency. "Competition know the deal, you're not ready now. / Because you're dealing with the R, know how it's going down." Here I'm basically saying that if you're so sick, where are your skills? "No sir, ghostwriter, you can kill that." So I'm really breaking it down very exactly. "The hood give my rap flow names, / like 9/11 and crack cocaine" is one of my favorite lines in that song. And "I hit the building, it get hotter in 'em. / It's like birds, most rappers don't know how to flip 'em" is another favorite line. The best of all, though, is when I put three metaphors in one phrase: "Gotta hip 'em, get hop . . . / I bus a rhyme and I school 'em for free, I scholarship 'em." It's a great example of metaphors and wordplay with different syllables: "Gotta hip 'em, . . . / I bus a rhyme and I school 'em for free, I scholarship 'em . . . / It's hard, this intricate flippin' it, / it isn't bars, it's infinite. So Ra deliver it far different."

I think of wordplay as playing drums with words. It's fun sometimes to take a few multi-syllable words and play drums, making the syllables implement the beat and making the beat sound different with the flow. It's also one of the ways I show my skill. I can take three- or four-syllable words and, in the first four bars, place them in a certain order. However, I sequence my rhymes. I'll place similar-sounding multi-syllable words somewhere different on the beat. In the first couple of bars, I might start a word on the one: *boom*, boom, boom. But then when I want to switch it up, I might come in on the second beat: boom, *boom*, boom. You take a breath and start it a little later or start it a little earlier, and what that does is it implements the beat a little differently. It'll be, *Duh, duh, duh, Duh, duh, duh, Duh, duh, duh, Duh, duh, duh* (123, 123, 123, 123). You take a breath and start it a little later or start it a little earlier, and what that does is it implements the beat a little different.

"Flow Forever" is another great example of a song with multi-syllable wordplay: "Whoever witnessed rapport like this before. / It's major, kiss the floor, say Bismillah. / It's the chosen one with the golden tongue. / Flow for the old and young, when I'm holding one. / In the front row city / we show no pity, where kids get jiggy. And you girls are so pretty. / The wanderer back from Casablanca / the conqueror, what next for Ra to conquer." I moved the words up a little bit, but it's the same three beats. Whatever the pattern of words I was using earlier, it's the same. I just moved it back.

It's all wordplay to me: laying the words to different parts of the beat, saying words that are so similar to each other or sound alike, using a word two or three times in the rhyme, in which the context changes the meaning of the word every time it's used, and putting certain words around each other and in a different order to make them sound different or give them a certain rhythm. I always try to have fun with it.

FIND YOUR PATH

Whatever your path in life becomes within or beyond your artistic aspirations, finding your purpose provides your starting point and your direction. It sounds simple, and, for some, it is staring you in the face. You could be born into it. When I watch videos of LeBron James's son playing basketball, it's hard for me to imagine that the game is not in his genes and that his purpose must be to be a ballplayer. Similarly, when you witness Serena and Venus Williams dominate not just a court but their entire lifestyle, they appear so empowered to the purpose of being not just tennis players but champions. Outside of sports, another idol of mine, Bruce Lee, was born in the year and hour of the dragon, to a father who was a successful entertainer and a mother from a prominent cross-cultural business family. He developed his skills through lessons and practice, but it's hard to believe his purpose and power to break down cultural barriers and forge an iconic entertainment career were not instilled before practicing Wing Chun.

Finding purpose can be a soul-searching journey to discover your driving force, possibly leading you in directions you may not have initially considered. I was really young when I fell in love with hip-hop, but by the time I started to rap I had already loved football all of my life. I can barely remember a time when I wasn't obsessed with the game. As a high school player, I enjoyed enough success on the field to think about playing in college. Hip-hop in those days was more like a hobby. And while young Black kids growing up in the hood saw professional sports as something to aspire to, hip-hop had not yet made that ascension. By the time it became clear to me that football wasn't in my future, I was on my path to hip-hop—my purpose for being on this Earth. It grew out of my identity: my spiritual focus at an early age, my laid-back personality, my growing up in a musical family, my love of watching the reactions to my performance and, later, instilling messages in my rhymes that made people not just clap but think. All of these variables led me to find purpose in hip-hop. Rapping, for me, became much more than a hobby once I realized that it connected me to my purpose. This understanding led me to think about how I could nurture my voice as an artist who wants to spread consciousness.

Having a purpose helps give you creative direction. It's what separates you and puts you on your path. It gives you almost a sixth sense that you're following your passion for a reason, and it helps you stay focused.

We all are individuals. We all experience different things. A lot of people become artists for different reasons. Sometimes your purpose is to bring out new styles, to push the genre, your field. Over time, your purpose is instinctive. To me, having a sense of purpose makes everything I'm experiencing on this Earth more important. Some people might say, "You're just a rapper!" They might think rapping has no purpose: go to the studio, do shows, and get money. But I find that I value my craft even more because I believe this is my purpose. Of course this means thinking about how I can get better. Once I realized I had a talent for rapping and my life purpose was connected to hip-hop, I began to sharpen my focus on how I could improve my craft. Three keys guided me: originality; the vibrations in the music; and the challenge to always be better than myself.

ORIGINALITY

In the early days, originality was part of the hip-hop ethos—a distinctive style was part of any rapper's identity. Originality speaks volumes for artists and writers at all levels. Sometimes discovering who you are and what makes you unique helps you to find your style. What comes from your mind makes your art different from everybody else's. Take advantage of that. It's what attracts people to your art. Too often emerging artists prefer to go with the norm. The result is that repetition in art, music, etc., becomes normal—until someone is able to change up the tempo. Often audiences are attracted to the unusual. Don't be afraid to find that in your work. Use that to make people stop and look and listen. A lot of the time people can't find their own style or purpose because they're too busy trying to be someone else. Individuality is what makes someone uniquely interesting. A person who knows how to project individuality is going to go a long way.

You have to motivate yourself to be the best. And one way of doing this is to be original and different. Try to go beyond what everybody is doing right now. Sometimes it could be with a concept:

> *Astray into the Milky Way, world's out of sight.*
> *Far as the eye could see, not even a satellite.*
> *Now stop and turn around and look.*
> *As you stare into darkness, your knowledge is took!*

When I wrote that for "Follow the Leader," no other rapper was explaining how they could whip every other MC's ass in one round by taking their opponents into the stars! New concepts. Sometimes new rhythms. New ways. Sometimes just a new, ill word. Always push yourself to bring something fresh, something that makes people excited.

Try to find your own lane, then stay in your own lane and stay focused. It's always easier to express yourself with your own art than to try to do what somebody else is doing with their art. There are always different things artists can do, but perfect your path. And you're always going to get people saying you should do this, you should do that, you should try this, you should . . . You can try a whole bunch of things, but you can't do everything. If you've identified your style and the direction you're going, only you know that. And it's not a good idea to have too many people in your ear who may detour you from your approach.

VIBRATIONS IN THE MUSIC

You can see it like it was yesterday. That's the good thing about good music, classic music. When you hear a song now that you heard in your youth, you have no idea what it did to you that day—even as it's taking you right now back to that first day when you heard it. But if it hadn't affected you then, you wouldn't be having any of the memories that come to mind as you hear it now. The music hits you almost like it could put everything in slow motion. Because when it hits a nerve, it heightens your awareness. Music is vibration, and when it hits a certain spot, it boosts your energy. And it gives you a photo-flash memory of that moment. That's why you remember it: something happened that transformed you. It's like your first kiss. You remember that? Do you remember right where you were when you heard a certain song when it came out? I can hear certain songs playing now, and they bring to mind the scent of my mom's perfume. Certain records can make me feel like I'm sitting in the car, going over to my cousin's crib. Good music makes you sit back and think of something, but it's not like you're straining to remember it. Some things are logged in your memory, but with music it's more than just a memory. With music, you don't have to strain. When the music comes on, it's like *bang* and you're there. And you can't even back out of that moment, that feeling, until it finishes with you. And you can't deny it. Once you hear art, you have no say. It's going to do one or two things to you. It's going to hit that nerve and make you appreciate it. Or if it's a song you don't like, you may not appreciate it.

I'll listen to any kind of music if it's a well-put-together song. It doesn't have to be hip-hop. It doesn't have to be R&B or jazz—any kind of music. If it's a well-put-together song and it's good, I have no control to not like it. I might say, "Oh, this is some real garbage we're listening to right now. Change the station," but my foot is tapping. I might even get mad that I like it: "They got me dancing to this? Turn the station!" Nah, it's all right. Tap to it. It's music. It's healing you. That's why you get happy and start tapping and dancing and singing. Because you feel good, and it's healing. When you are at a party and your friends are dancing and having fun, you almost have no choice but to tap your foot, sing, dance, clap, smile. It's natural.

Looking back, I can definitely say that the music, the samples I chose to rhyme over, served multiple purposes. It all helped to create that signature Rakim style. It created that flow. And for each song I rapped over, it was the music that made me say what I said. When I first started rhyming, I would write rhymes and rhyme over the beat. But as I perfected the craft, I stopped doing that because I wanted to wait to see how the music was going to make me feel—and that feeling, created by the music, is what began to inspire my creativity and shape my style.

ALWAYS BE BETTER THAN YOURSELF

I started realizing early on that one of the best ways to improve was simply to be better than myself. One of my earliest memories of this was when Eric B. and I first started going into the studio to make albums. Eric B.'s brother, Ant Live, was one of a handful of folks close to us who used to be at all the sessions.

Ant Live said to me one day, "Yo, I know it's hard trying to outdo yourself." I believe we were working on the *Follow the Leader* album at the time. He was one of these cool, laid-back cats who generally kept a straight face. I looked at him when he said this, and he busted out laughing. "Yo, man. I get it. You want everything to be better than the last record you did." Ant basically listened to every song. He was like my unofficial A&R person, one of the few people I wanted in the studio to give us feedback on how they liked the music we were creating. We didn't have A&Rs for the first four albums.

He was right. That's what I was thinking. He'd put it into words, said it out loud, and made me think more about it. Of course I'm trying to just get better and better. But the way he'd said it also let me know unequivocally who my competition was at that time.

You have to understand what's going on in the industry. But your ultimate goal is to put yourself in a position where you're your only competition, and the only way you can do that is to pick your own lane and do something that's innovative and original. When you can do that, you don't have to reinvent yourself. You can keep making music because it doesn't matter what any other artist puts out. You're not competing with that. You're competing with the last thing you did. That's one way of sticking to your guns and letting who you are speak through your work.

My man Ant Live! He used to keep me focused. Good cat. He was one of the dudes I could always ask honestly, "Yo, how that sound?"

"I think you should do that one over," he would say sometimes, giving me a thumbs-down. "You can do that better."

"All right. Take it from the top." Then, "How'd that sound?"

"Come on out, Yo. Put the headphones down and come out."

When I did "Paid in Full," I did just one verse and came out and sat down to start writing the second verse.

Ant was the first one to say, "Yo, leave it just like that. You ain't gotta do nothing else with that."

"Word, Ant? You think that was on point?"

"Trust me. It's done. You went through the whole story. That's the end of the story. It's done. Hit the studio. You paid in full. What else are you saying? It's done."

That was my thumbs-up.

THE GRIFFINS

My brother Stevie used to throw parties in our backyard, and he'd have the DJ set up on the patio. One night they let me rap a little. I was ten and I was getting really nice with it.

"That sounded all right, Poppo!" my mom exclaimed afterward. I could really feel her pride when she said that, and it gave me a jolt of energy. I felt like she believed in me, and that made me believe in me. After that, I made it my business to know everyone in Wyandanch who had recording equipment in their crib. I talked my way into their houses and made tapes as often as I could. I wasn't trying to become a rapper. I just enjoyed doing it. Every time I came home with a new tape, Mom would either ask to hear it or just hang around outside my door listening as I played it for myself. I never cursed in my music because I knew the first person to hear the song was going to be Mom. She always had comments and compliments that were encouraging and inspired me to keep going. She wasn't like that with everyone. Mom was from Brooklyn, and she said whatever she felt, no sugarcoating, so if she was telling me I was good, then it must be true.

Moms was the rock. A truly beautiful soul and she had the music gene. She was a trained opera singer who would also sing jazz, R&B, and everything in between. She once performed at the Apollo Amateur Night and finished second—they said she sounded too much like the great Sarah Vaughan. But she'd sung a Sarah Vaughan song so she was fine with that. Moms had the ear, she was a real musician, and hearing her sing around the house was really nice. It made me feel like she passed the music gene down to me.

I used to be so moved listening to the records she played. Growing up in that house, I soaked in everyone else's styles and got a deep understanding of music. And I got a ton of encouragement. Throughout my childhood, my whole family made me feel like I was good at everything I tried to do musically. No matter what I played or rapped, my family was always there to support me. Especially Mom. She was my biggest supporter. She was always there to encourage me, whether I was playing saxophone in school or headlining at Madison Square Garden or just listening to a new tape in my room.

Music was always playing in our house. It was in the DNA of my family. Moms had jazz in heavy rotation on the turntable: Miles Davis, Ella Fitzgerald, Cannonball Adderley. She made music seem important. I remember she'd start crying when certain songs came on, and I'd think, *Some songs can shake people to their soul.*

If Moms wasn't playing something, she was singing in the living room, or my brothers were down in the basement playing piano or sax, or my sisters were up in their room vocalizing, or I was doing my thing. My dad couldn't sing, but he was a jazz aficionado who also managed a couple of groups, including my brother Ronnie's R&B group the Magna-Tones. Ronnie, aka Ronald Griffin, the first born, studied the piano in grad school. He's a really serious musician. He's helped me with bass lines sometimes, but he was so intense when he played on my records that I had to work to get him to relax.

"Ronnie, take your left hand and put that it in your pocket. A hip-hop bass line doesn't need that many notes!" My brother is brilliant, but when it came to appealing to the emerging youth culture, sometimes I had to ask him to slow down to catch up.

Once Ronnie was down in the basement going wild on the piano, lifting the instrument with his knees as he worked the pedals. I was just sitting there watching him in amazement. I was seven, and he was twenty-one.

Then, while he kept on playing, he yelled at me, "Pick up the horn!"

I grabbed my brother Stevie's sax. "For what?" I didn't know what to do.

"Improvise!"

"What?"

"Play any notes you want!"

I started playing whatever came to me, and Ronnie cheered me on. "Keep going!"

It was the first time we played music together, and it was a thrill. It felt like he was pulling me into the world of music making.

After that, any time Stevie went out, I ran down to the basement and played his sax. After a few weeks of blowing on it, I started getting nice and could play anything from memory that I'd heard Stevie play. When I was young, I was always trying to be like Stevie, so if he played sax, I played the sax. Stevie was the middle child of us five kids, seven years older than me, and for a long time he and I shared a room. The whole place was glow-in-the-dark posters and black light because that's what Stevie liked. He loved being a little different and a little more creative. He was the type to get the biggest boom box in the hood and walk down the street blasting Parliament-Funkadelic's early rock-and-roll-type joints while wearing mismatched sneakers on purpose. He loved going against the grain, and he showed me how important it was to pick my own lane and never follow people. I always wanted to be like that.

For months I hid my sax playing from Stevie, until one day I cracked the reed. I didn't know anything about reeds or how to change them, but I knew I'd done something wrong. So I gently placed the sax back on its stand and ran off to my room to hide.

Next thing I knew, I heard Stevie yelling. He was mad. When he asked me, "Yo, did you break my reed?" I said nothing. "Were you messing with my saxophone?"

Moms ran in. "Don't yell at him, Stevie! He's good on that horn."

"What?" Stevie asked in disbelief.

"What?" I added, surprised that she had noticed.

"He can play exactly what you can," Mom said.

"Get outta here!" Stevie said. He put in a new reed and gave me the horn, and I blew it just like he did. He was so impressed that he gave me a hug. After that he gave me his sax all the time to help me get better.

Stephanie is my oldest sister, the second born. She also used to sing every day. She mostly chose what I thought of as tearjerkers, but I loved listening to her.

Sometimes she was called on to be a bit of the matriarch, and since I didn't like taking orders from anyone but my mother and father, that meant we'd bump heads. Once when I was six she was babysitting me. I said I wanted to go outside, and she said, "Okay, just don't go in the street." I listened to her, but she didn't tell me not to go around back, so that's where I went, and she completely lost sight of me. Next thing she knew, I was gone, and a car skidded in front of the house with a huge screech. She ran out in a panic, tears starting to stream down her face, and when she found me, safe and sound but not really where I should have been, she reeled back and slapped me across the face.

She yelled at me through her tears, "You could've gotten hurt!" she said.

"I'm hurt now! Stop slapping me," I said.

"Shut up!"

An hour later, Mom was about to come home, and I still had a big red welt on my face right where Steph had slapped me.

"Oh God, Mommy's gonna kill me!" Steph said, looking at me, visibly shaken.

"Don't worry," I said. "I won't say you did it. I don't want you to get in trouble."

"Awww! Thank you, Pop," she said, hugging me. "That's really sweet."

"But," I said, "after Mom gets back, can you go to the store and get me some candy?"

"Um, okay."

That's when it started. Whenever I wanted something I'd buzz by Steph's room. "Can I have five dollars?" "Can you get me a soda?" "Can you get me some candy?"

I kept it going for a while. Stephanie called it blackmail, but I called it keeping her from getting in trouble with Mom. After a year of me steadily picking her pocket, she said, "I don't care if you tell Mom. I can't afford you no more!"

I took a little advantage of what was really just her love and concern, but in a bit of a devious, roundabout way, it made me realize that I might have been the youngest, but I wasn't completely powerless. She probably didn't appreciate it at the time, but she helped me grow a little closer to being my own man.

Robin is the fourth born and closest to me in age. She was the last babysitter I ever had, and she was considered the smartest of us all, the bookworm who was always getting As and Bs in school. When I started writing rhymes, I would often use words I wasn't sure about the meaning of, and Robin was my fact checker and sounding board. When I was a little older, I was sitting at home writing one of the first songs I would professionally record, and I wanted to use the word "majesty," but I wasn't sure if it was used to describe a king or a queen. Robin told me it stood for royal power and sometimes for dignified beauty. It fit perfectly into the bar: "My strategy has to be tragedy, catastrophe, and after this you'll call me your majesty. My melody."

TRUE MEANING

I was in the third grade and it was just three weeks until Christmas. Time to ask big. Moms gave me the Sears catalog and told me to circle what I wanted, and if it was something I really wanted, I could put a star and a check by it. I circled, starred, and checked two turntables, a mixer, and four speakers.

"I don't know if what you see around here is confusing you, but we ain't rich," Mom said.

I guess I kinda thought we were. We had a two-story house with a basement, a nice front yard, and a pool in the back. I got most of the things I asked for and never worried about money.

Mom rattled off a series of questions that made me wonder if my DJ'ing aspirations hung in the balance: "You want to have equipment with no electricity to run it because we can't pay the light bill? You want to DJ on an empty stomach?" But a year later, my parents got me my own turntables.

Mom worked as a nurse and my father was a mechanic and entrepreneur who periodically ran small businesses. He'd owned a sneaker store called Willie's and done lots of side gigs, like running food trucks and managing singing groups. He could fix anything—people called him at home all the time and told him what was wrong with their car and how it sounded, and just from listening, he'd tell them how to fix it. A minute later they'd come zipping into our driveway to say thanks. He worked as a mechanic at Blue Comet, where they fixed big trucks, and for American Airlines at John F. Kennedy International Airport, about a half hour's drive from our house. When I went to work with him, we walked through the gates and back corridors of the airport, going through back doors and stepping over tires. When he got around the other mechanics, I saw how much respect he commanded. As soon as he sat down, someone came running into his office to ask for help. Pops stood up, grabbed a wrench that was three feet long, and walked under a 747 where all the panels were open, and you could see all the wires and guts of the thing, millions of bolts and screws.

"See that right there?" my father said, right off the rip. "That's your problem. You gotta take that out, and while you're at it, replace that right there too. Both of them are about to go."

My father used to practice shooting targets in the basement. He loved his guns. My uncles would come over and see who could shoot the sharpest or draw the fastest. My father usually won.

Pops had a way of saying things without being completely straightforward. He talked in a way that cloaked his meaning. Once I asked him for money, and when he gave it to me he said, "Squeeze the green off." I thought he meant don't lose it, so I held on to it tight until I got to the store and spent all of it. I didn't understand until years later that he meant don't spend it quickly. He was telling me to hold on to it so long that the ink would come off on my fingers.

He loved to say some things that left me wondering what he

really meant. What he wanted to do was make me think, make me work a little to figure out his meaning. When I started training for football, I'd run to school and back, until one day he said, "Why don't you run backwards?" I looked at him like . . . *What?* The next morning I realized what he meant. I was a quarterback and most of the time quarterbacks run backwards. He was always talking like that, and it made me want to talk like that too.

My father was my hero who stood proudly beside me whenever I achieved a milestone on the way to being a better person. But he was no doubt the man of the house. If I did something dumb, he let me know that as well.

Once, when I was nine, he told me several times to rake the leaves in the yard. I kept procrastinating and saying, "Don't worry, I'll do it later," and for a little while he would let me slide.

Then one Saturday morning he went to the hardware store and got a new rake and put it in my hands. "You've told me a hundred times you are going to take care of the leaves," he said. "Luckily, I just bought you a brand-new rake."

Procrastination was over.

I stepped out and got to it, but the rake kept catching on the wire fence that enclosed the garden. Each time it caught, I'd yank it a little harder, just letting out a little frustration at being stuck doing chores.

Pops saw me fighting with the rake. He knew I wanted to be anywhere but in the yard doing work.

"Let me show you how to do that," he said. He showed me how to rake so it wouldn't get caught in the fence.

I started again, and two minutes later it got caught again, but this time when I yanked it out, it broke.

My father came running over. "You broke my new rake?"

Before I could even react, he pulled back and punched me dead center in the chest—*boom!* A short, stiff right hand to the heart. Hit me so hard my chest kind of wrapped around his fist. As I gasped for air, he walked off. When he came back, I had that yard raked perfectly. I recognized I'd had one too many chances to just do what he'd asked.

Another time, my father got me some sneakers as a gift, but they were what we called growing up "skips"—virtually brandless, plain, canvas, and, most importantly to me, insignificant when it came to status at school. Wack. I had asked for Chuck Taylors, the classics, but instead I got Chuck Taylor knockoffs. At that age and in my mind, I couldn't be seen on the block with these. I'd be laughed at forever.

I took those skips outside, found a nail, and poked a big hole in one of them. Ripped it right open. I went back inside through the kitchen door to where my parents were seated at the dining room table and made a dramatic entrance.

"My shoe got ripped," I announced.

"Take that shoe off," my father replied incredulously. He looked at the hole for one entire second. "Ain't no way this happened accidentally. The hole goes all the way through. You cut that sneaker up on purpose. Probably with a nail. Am I wrong?"

My whole world crumbled. I hardly ever lied to anyone, but least of all to Willie Griffin.

My silence told him all he needed to know.

"Wait right here. I'm gonna get Suzy."

Suzy had been part of the family since before I was born. She was originally a leather strap used to sharpen blades at a barber shop, but he had fashioned it into something to whip his kids with. When we really crossed a line and messed up, my father got Suzy, and we sat and walked funny for a week.

I heard him open the drawer that he kept Suzy in, and my knees buckled. I started to cry. He whacked my butt hard three hard times with that strap, and it hurt so bad I felt like my ass had been electrified. I couldn't take one more lick from Suzy. I had to confess and tell him I had ruined the sneakers on purpose. As soon as I admitted that, he stopped. He put away the strap and went out. About an hour later, he came back to the house with a new pair of Chuck Taylors. The shoes I had really wanted. Pops was tough on me, but I always knew that he loved me.

INSPIRATION

Mahogany

Me and Eric B. was cooling at the Palladium
Seen an all world covered girl, I said, "Hey, lady, I'm
Sorry if you're in a rush. Don't let me hold ya up
Or intervene or interrupt, but
you got the look, I wanna get to know ya better
I had to let her know, but yo, I didn't sweat her
'Cause if you woulda seen what I was seein'
Almost looked Korean, but European.
When she spoke, her accent was self-explanatory.
Even her body language told the story.
Her name was Mahogany, twin's name was Ebony.
I said, "My name is Ra and this is Eric B."
Since the music was loud, I said, "Let's take a walk,"
So we could talk and see New York.
"Showtime didn't start until one o'clock"
But once I entered your mind I wouldn't wanna stop
Caress your thoughts till we was thinkin' the same
Calm your nerves, massage your brain

Each moment's a mineral, poetry is protein
Verse is a vitamin affects like codeine.
Now tell me how you feel and I'll reveal
A pill that'll heal your pain 'cause I'm real.
She musta OD'ed 'cause she couldn't resist.
She spoke slowly when she told me this, she said

[Hook]

Over me, she was going crazy.
She'll rub me on my chest and call me Mr. Sexy.
She said she want my kids and help me make my next G
Tell me I ain't finesse, Mahogany . . .
So I prescribed her something to revive her
Surprise her, she's live-er and much more wiser
From the light I shine when the brain cells spark,
Constantly so she can glow in the dark
Then soon you can represent the moon
As long as I keep you in tune
I'll tell you who you are and why you're here
Take it in stride 'cause it might take a year.
It's funny how time flies when your having fun.
We got close and it was almost one.
She kissed me slow, but you know how far a kiss can go
F*ck around and miss the show.
So I told her to hold that thought real tight,
We can finish where we left off later on tonight
Back to the scene of the crime on time
As they introduced the fiend of a rhyme
She stood in the crowd with a bird's-eye view of me

Thinking of later on, of what she would do to me

The back of the room I could see her eyes gloom

Patient, but hoping that the show was over soon.

As the place was ripped in half, she made her way to the
   front row

So I said, "Let's go."

I packed my mic as they screamed for an encore.

The speakers were blown, plus my mic was sore.

Besides I got places to go, ladies to see,

and she could tell me how crazy she was over me.

We drove off, she said she liked the way that I performed.

And couldn't wait to get "soft and warm." I said,

"I was watchin' you watchin' me.

Looks I received made it hard to MC.

I can take a hint, so I knew that she

wanted my agony, agony, agony in her body.

Showed her some sights, then I took her to the condo.

She was pipin' hot, but I kept my calm so

She asked how come I don't smile.

I said, "Everything's fine, but I'm in a New York state of mind!"

As we reached the kingdom, she said bring some

Champagne, she'll entertain then sing some

sentimental songs real gentle.

It hit the spot and you know where it went to.

As we embraced I felt her heart pumpin'.

I knew she was in the mood for somethin'.

So I laid on my back and relaxed.

It wasn't the Pérignon

that made her collapse.

[Hook]

Over me, she's going crazy.
She'll rub me on my chest and call me Mr. Sexy.
She said she want my kids and help me make my next G
Tell me I ain't finesse, Mahogany.

Notes on "Mahogany"

When I first started recording songs in an actual studio, this was my process: lay the beat, at least to the point where it's almost done, then take out a pad and start writing. Maybe two hours in, I would have the lyrics done. Then I'd go right into the booth and read my rhyme, and lay it onto the record. Back then we were so young and excited. There was no manual, so that became the recipe.

Looking back on the process now, I feel that rather than reading your words, it's better to memorize them. To own them. It allows you to take control of your work. If there's one thing I would have done differently on those early songs, that's it. You can emphasize certain points of a song and put feeling in other parts, instead of trying to read and make sure you're staying on beat. Reading takes away from your expression.

However being in a studio means you can lay down a beat, get everything crystal clear and mixed to the highest quality then, right at the point of completion, take that excitement and jump right in the booth, lyrics fresh on your mind, samples still spinning and the ink barely dry in your notebook. Nothing could match the feeling, the sense of urgency and immediacy of finishing a song and at that moment flexing: "I'm going into the booth."

We did a lot of songs that way. Sometimes Eric B. would come in with an idea and lay it down. I came in a couple of times and the beat was already done, which was dope. All I had to do was get comfortable, take out the notebook, and get started. "Mahogany" is an example of a song we did that way. It was one of those songs that gave me a chance to talk to the ladies.

As a writer, I draw inspiration from a variety of places. For example, when I got my first car, I was still living on Long Island, and I would drive into New York City. Coming out of Long Island on the Grand Central Parkway headed toward the Triborough Bridge, the closer you get, you start seeing the Manhattan skyline. My favorite buildings in those days were the Twin Towers. I used to go as slow as possible so I could take it all in. I would let my imagination run wild about what was going on all over the city, just by looking at the skyline. Later on, when I moved into Manhattan, some of the activity I'd observe on the streets would inspire me in the same way. I'd create pieces of stories or sometimes whole narratives from some of the everyday things I'd see on the streets. It might be a guy down on his luck, pushing a shopping cart around filled with who knows what. *What happened in his life before he reached this point?* It might be a young lady looking good with a great outfit and a little bit of attitude in her walk. You can look at a lady and know that she's on a certain level and that starts to paint a picture: a no-nonsense sister, works every day, not messing with broke dudes. It's evident. Look at the way she's dressed. Her head is on straight—a well-put-together lady. So how does she spend her day and what makes her happy or angry or what's it take to make her fall in love?

"Mahogany" was also inspired by the movie *Mahogany*, which starred Diana Ross. I loved that movie, and I loved Diana Ross. I also liked the way the word "mahogany" expressed the word "Black" in a different way. *Mahogany*. When I first heard it, I remember thinking, *Damn! That's a dope-ass name.* The film came out in 1975 and was about a star coming up and facing adversities and struggles, personal problems, demons that she had to deal with. Basically, it's about what a lot of artists and stars go through that the general public doesn't experience up close and personal. Most people think that once you have success as a celebrity entertainer, everything is good. They think that if you're in that situation, you shouldn't have any problems. But money doesn't mean happiness. Money is means. It allows you to do some things you wouldn't otherwise be able to do, but it doesn't necessarily make you happy about everything. *Mahogany* is one of those movies that gives you a front-row seat to see inside the life of a celebrity.

When Eric B. and I were working on our third album, *Let the Rhythm Hit 'Em*, I remember sitting and thinking I wanted to do a song for the ladies. The idea for the song popped into my head, but it wasn't until I was already writing it and trying to settle on a name for the woman I met in the rhyme that I decided to name it "Mahogany," largely because of the way the film and Diana Ross's music moved me. Fun song, witty song, and it resonated with both the men and the ladies. It was a cool story and vivid, so it came off well. To this day, it's a dope song that I love to perform.

Mike D., one of our boys we met hanging out in Power Play Studios back in the day, brought us the beat for "Mahogany" already done. "Mahogany" sampled Al Green's "I'm Glad You're Mine." (The Average White Band's song "School Boy Crush" was another one of the beats he brought us.) When we were working on *Follow the Leader*, he said, "Y'all gotta do this joint, both of these joints—Al Green and the Average White Band," Mike exclaimed, in a way that suggested he just knew we were going to love it.

Since the Average White Band's song was called "School Boy Crush," I wanted to do my crush: the microphone. But I didn't want to call it "Microphone Crush." So I called it "Microphone Fiend." That was my way of keeping the title similar to the original title but still adding that hip-hop flavor to it. "Microphone Fiend" recounts my experience as a young rapper obsessed and in love with MC'ing. I mention kicking holes in speakers and pulling out plugs, which was basically me retelling a moment of my childhood going to Wyandanch Park. I didn't realize at that time how ridiculous it was to think these guys would listen to me. But now I can imagine a little eight-year-old kid approaching the booth and asking a DJ spinning at a party if he can rap. The DJ would probably laugh. "Yo, somebody get this little kid out of here before he falls and hurts himself. Whose son is this?" But when I was that young, I didn't think anything of it. I just wanted to rap. Certain people in the neighborhood would let me get on the mic. But I got laughed at a few times. "Come on, Shorty. Back up from the ropes." *Okay, I'll back up from the ropes, all right.* I'd walk right over to the bathrooms in the park where they plugged in their equipment, politely kick the plug out, and then make my escape by running over to the basketball courts. I did that on a few occasions. In "Microphone Fiend" I was speaking to that kid who couldn't get on the mic and I was saying, *Look how far you've come.* It might not sound like a touch-your-heart sort of record to you, but it was to me.

As I wrote "Microphone Fiend," I was still reaching for ways to be innovative. The song starts not with beat-boxing but with "Ahem ha ahem ha-ha-ha-ha." That was my James Brown. I used to love the way James Brown emphasized grunts and moans, put accents on beats, and sounded so funky. So that was my little "Arung-ah," without screaming "Arrghhhhhhh!" and without totally just stealing his style. That was my way of peppering the beat up.

James Brown had a really big influence on the way I thought hip-hop should sound. First of all, he was rapping before we were. Add to that the way he was doing his music: the drums on his tracks, the way the horns would hit, the way he would scream. I used to try to imagine what he was thinking when he was making his music. Nobody was doing that back in the day. He invented that, and he just brought his own style—even the way he danced! Incredible. I'm amazed by people who do things first and do it so good. "Who showed you how to do that?" "Where did you get that from?" I admired people like that and studied their craft so I could learn how to do the same thing with hip-hop. I wanted to create something no one had done before, do it effortlessly, and make it so amazing that other people couldn't help but try to emulate it—if not outright steal it. I wanted to create an approach so original and distinctive that anyone else doing it would immediately say, "That's Rakim style."

FIND INSPIRATION TO BE GREAT

We are good at birth. Everyone has a clean slate. Not only that, generally speaking, we all begin with a pretty equal amount of skill, talent, or know-how—meaning we are born to be good. We all have some amount of common sense. But common sense will only take you so far. What comes after that is the difference between good artists and great artists. Being good is one thing, but you have to push yourself to be great.

In the beginning it was easy to inspire myself. I was only eighteen when I did my first album, but I felt like I had a much older and wiser level of worldly understanding. One of the privileges of being the youngest in the family was absorbing all the lessons and experiences that I could from my moms and pops, my brothers and sisters, and my aunts, uncles, and endless friends. I had ten to fifteen years of information and creativity balled up inside me. Now I had to make a quantum leap to surpass what I had done to first gain recognition.

I remember knowing what I had to do, but not knowing

where to start—anxious to reach the next level, but not knowing how to get there. No idea. Once I owned being an artist, I started to focus on ways to become better. After I did that, everything I took for granted began to take on a new significance: life, a beautiful day, a day on the water, the view from the top of a building, a kind word from someone, something I didn't believe I could do that I finally accomplished. Suddenly a blade of grass growing out of the ground was not so boring. Suddenly a bee pollinating a flower became more interesting. Babies being born. Existence. Studying became exploration and listening to music was interactive research.

I began to see that *everything* was inspiration.

My journey into the world of music began at home. As a kid, I wanted to go outside and play kickball with my friends, not dig in the crates just yet. But there was good music being brought into the house. First, it was what my mother and father picked. After that, it was anything my brothers and sisters were listening to. Once I realized that music was important in our household, I gravitated toward it. The Griffins had a special connection to music, maybe even a talent for it, and I had to fall in line. I fell in love with the music they fell in love with.

I remember being inspired by music like the Pointer Sisters' "Yes We Can Can" and Marvin Gaye's "What's Going On?," which made me feel like I could do it too. Music always influenced me to a great degree. Even in my earliest days of getting on the mic, I took a little bit of inspiration from my favorite artists, along with the way the music made me feel, then I used that as fuel to drive creation. John Coltrane. Stevie Wonder. Ray Charles. Johann Sebastian Bach. My aunt

Ruth Brown, a Rock and Roll Hall of Fame inductee whose voice, energetic style, and innovation earned her the name the "Queen of R&B." As I thought more about that quantum leap, I began to draw inspiration from many different artists and listened to all kinds of music that made me want to push myself further, everything from jazz to R&B to hip-hop to rock and roll to opera to classical.

I discovered many other talented and amazing people—inside and outside of the world of art, icons in the pages of history, in spiritual practice, in general everyday observations, and those emerging in news headlines—who were operating at the top of their game. Studying their practices and rituals made me begin to imagine that I could be remembered like some of these cats were remembered for pushing themselves to the limits of greatness. Among them were politicians, activists, military leaders, entertainers, athletes, spiritual leaders, and more:

- The world's greatest entertainer was James Brown. Hands down. His music and his dancing and his showmanship set the standard. Michael Jackson took the dance and everything James Brown was doing to another level with his stage production and more. But sometimes it's not about having the best voice or being the greatest singer or performer. A great example is Frank Sinatra. Sinatra just felt genuine. He was able to use his voice and put his songs together in such a way that he came across as a regular person who knew how to sing. Nobody can do what he did the way he did it. And when I listen to his singing today, there's still that special something about it. Listen to "Fly Me to the Moon." The scene that it painted was so dope. Something about Frank Sinatra's approach takes you on a journey. "In other words, please be true. In other words, I love you." You can sit back and see the moment in time. When you hear it, you can envision the canvas as Frank was painting it: the band in a smoke-filled room, him on a stage, sitting or standing, drink in one hand, cigarette in the other. He was the biggest star at the time, but he made people feel as if he was just like them. On a stage, standing casually with a drink and a cigarette and talking to the people, he bridged the gap between the performer and the audience. It's that same connection I remember experiencing sitting with my mom at home watching him, Sammy Davis, and Dean Martin on television. One of the main things that stood out was how they interacted with the crowd in a way that made people feel closer to the entertainers. That was the first time I saw singers stop and dialogue with an audience.

- There is no better inspiration than what you draw from reality that gives you substance, reason, and meaning. Martin Luther King Jr., Malcolm X, and John F. Kennedy were some of the people I looked up to when I was a young boy becoming more politically and culturally aware. I admired their courage to put their lives on the line for something they were passionate about and for the good of other people. That's real life.

- Because I played football in high school, Walter Payton and Roger Staubach are two great NFL athletes who inspired me. Later on, the NBA all-time great Michael Jordan was another inspiration. Part of Michael Jordan's appeal was that he was just so dominant. He pushed the envelope for sports in general, reaching the point when his brand exceeded basketball. No other athlete has ever done that. There are Jordan shoes for professional boxing. You can find football gear that has a Jordan logo on it. Jordan cleats for baseball. Never has a boxer worn the logo of a baseball player, but Jordan's brand is all over the place. He was so great at what he did that people want to achieve his level of greatness within their own area of expertise. He was definitely one of the biggest inspirations of my time.

- Elijah Muhammad's example of personal sacrifice is rooted in the fact that he brought something profound—knowledge of self and Islam—to black Americans at a time when ignorance and white racism were working overtime to keep the black race from moving forward. As founder of the Nation of Islam, Muhammad emerged and led this cultural awakening, influencing many people, including Nation of Islam ministers Malcolm X and Louis Farrakhan as well as Clarence 13X Smith, founder of the Five Percent Nation (also called the Nation of Gods and Earths).

- Minister Louis Farrakhan was an essential source of information when I worked on my *The Seventh Seal* album. I listen to his lectures and imagine how much he studies and how long he sits in a room and pulls so much information together and prepares it so succinctly. I find his capacity to condense complex ideas and make them accessible to the common man to be incredible. The ways he continues to build on Elijah Muhammad's legacy of Islam for blacks in the US makes him an unparalleled contemporary religious leader.

- General Hannibal of Carthage was one of the greatest military minds I read about in order to perfect my craft as an MC. His wars against the Roman Empire are legendary, and his strategies continue to be taught in military academies around the world. To this day, he is known as someone who did the impossible. During his time, having a big army was important. Hannibal didn't always have the most men. He didn't have the best weapons. But he had the most brilliant military strategies and the smartest tactics of anyone around at that time. What I learned from studying him was this: use your mind to create a master plan. Just as Hannibal is elevated for his contributions, dictators like Hitler, Idi Amin, and Benito Mussolini are examples of devious, demonic, manipulative leaders who were among the worst influences in world history. I mention them here not to celebrate evil but because it is essential to always pay attention to the entire spectrum of any arena, to turn over every rock and acknowledge the good, the bad, and the ugly, and all that each entails. You need a certain aggressiveness for rap. Aggression is also the forte of dictators. And just as the performer's goal is to persuade large groups of people to listen to and repeat their messages, buy their albums, and come to their concerts, these men influenced massive groups of people to commit gruesome atrocities. Even as you raise the question "How did they do that?" set limitations and find your moral center.

One of the cornerstones of inspiration is understanding the influence, both divine and devious, of all types of historical figures, whether they seem obvious to one's purpose and path or not. To limit oneself to the study of only your own discipline can stifle artistic progression when you must always strive to stimulate it. So a piano player should obviously research Mozart and Monk but also look to Moses and MacArthur and Spielberg and Sartre. Inspiration is everywhere, and to gain the knowledge required to become your best self and create your best work, seek inspiration not only in the obvious but across all spectrums of culture. In the effort to expand my thinking, elevate my creativity, and always outdo myself, I observe and record, and I learn from teachers, from books, from art, from science, from spirituality, from strangers on the street, and, many times most of all, from my closest family. Cultivating a constant and unquenchable thirst for the next spark of brilliance is the only way to cross the divide from good to great.

LEE AND ALI

I t was impossible to grow up in those days without being influenced by two real-life superheroes: the actor and martial-arts expert Bruce Lee and the heavyweight champion Muhammad Ali.

Bruce Lee was a young Hong Kong–American actor who blended his career in film with his passion for *Jeet Kune Do*, an approach to martial arts that he spearheaded. He might have been five foot seven, five foot eight, and have weighed about 140 pounds maybe, but he could whip the asses of dudes twice his size. The bulk of his films were made in the early 1970s, before he died in 1973, but soon after that, he gained a cultlike following among young Americans—especially among Black kids in the hood. Films he starred in, like *Fist of Fury*, *The Way of the Dragon*, and *Enter the Dragon*, were watched over and over and discussed endlessly by my friends and me. We examined every detail we could find out about him. His dedication to martial arts, the long hours and years he put into his training, and the various schools of thought he incorporated into his practice. Seeing the results in the dramatic fight scenes in his films, in which he generally dominated opponents, made us fall in love with the art form. It wasn't lost on us that Bruce Lee was just as mental as he was physical, and that he was able to be so physical because he used his mind to push himself to standards that went beyond all others. We watched in awe as he, again and again, vanquished all comers, whether they came by twos or threes or more. Some of us begged our parents to let us join karate classes, which were cropping up in the neighborhood at community centers and after-school programs. Others started imitating kicks and moves on each other that we saw Bruce Lee use in his films.

Sure, how he broke the laws of gravity, his willpower, his passion, and how spiritual and smart a fighter he was came to mind, when I thought about ways of perfecting my rhyme style. But as a little boy hanging out with friends and watching these films, I was simply amazed by the art and mastery of Bruce Lee kicking ass. One technique I learned from him was that you don't just throw your jab out there. If you want to really do damage, you throw that jab and you turn your fist. That way your knuckles scrape over your opponent's face the moment you make contact, which extends your impact. I incorporated that move into my fighting style in those days, on the playground or anywhere else we got into fistfights.

A reality star of sorts before reality television, Bruce Lee engaged fellow celebrities of his day, actors like Chuck Norris and John Saxon. Basketball star Kareem Abdul-Jabbar was mentored by Lee at one point and even appeared in one of his Hong Kong films.

Muhammad Ali was another one of the cats I was fascinated with—like damn near everybody else my age. He too was a popular icon even though he was nearing the end of his career by this time, with his first retirement announced in 1979. I was a huge fan and remember watching some of his fights on television, sitting on the floor next to my father.

I also remember one day watching a movie about him called *The Greatest*, which came out in 1977. I was in elementary school at the time, maybe fourth or fifth grade. I know I was pretty young because I didn't have a TV in my room yet. Back in the day, you had two TVs in the house, one in the living room and the other in your parents' room. You did not go in our living room, though. That was for our parents to entertain their friends and other adults.

I was glued to the TV, watching Ali's life story. As much as I enjoyed his boxing, what I remember most was learning for the first time about the stands he took and sacrifices he made outside the ring. Protesting the Vietnam War. Things he went through joining the Nation of Islam. Changing his name from Cassius Clay to Muhammad Ali. His friendship with Malcolm X. The respect he had for Elijah Muhammad. These new revelations gave me much more respect for him.

As the movie ended, the theme song "The Greatest Love of All" played, sung by George Benson: "I believe that children are the future. / Teach them well and let them lead the way. / Show them all the beauty they possess inside . . ." Listening to the notes and lyrics and still struck by Ali's story, I felt an emotional lump form in my stomach. The moment reminded me of my mom being moved to tears by some of her favorite songs. But now this movie and its theme song struck a nerve in me. I was still just a kid, but what I felt passionate about was starting to be revealed to me. Ali's dominance as an athlete was what initially drew me to him. But then I recognized that he stood for something more. At the same time, the music hit me, I realized who I was: I loved music and I was beginning to see that I felt a connection to the act of taking a principled stand. I identified with Martin Luther King Jr. and John F. Kennedy for the same reasons I loved Muhammad Ali. These were people who used their influence to empower others.

Later on, when I thought about developing my craft, the reasons why I admired Bruce Lee and Muhammad Ali came to mind. I wanted to emulate these brothers with the pen. It made it easier to convert inspiration to music—I wanted to create new ways of rhyming like they had come up with new ways of destroying all opponents. But I still didn't have an answer for how I could connect my love for music with my concern for uplift and the desire to see people empowered and doing better.

COMING UP

I came up block boxing dudes who really knew how to fight, so I got really nice with my hands. I was quick, fearless, and even though I was small, because I was taking notes from Bruce Lee and Muhammad Ali, I knew how to make my punches sting. I was always sparring with guys way older than me. When I was ten, I met a big fifteen-year-old named Ron Drew. He was diesel like iron and crazy as hell. He was bigger than me and tougher than me, but I moved faster than anyone out there, so when we put 'em up to test our skills, he couldn't catch me. I could zigzag inside his defense and whack him in the face and dance away. I amazed him. Before long, he took me under his wing. I started calling him I-Ron because he was so strong. He loved rapping, fighting, and cars, so we had a lot in common. Even though he was way older, we got to be really good friends. He even let me borrow his car sometimes. He was a true brother to me. We ran together for years.

One day me and I-Ron stopped at a store on our way to some party. An older cat pulled him aside. "Why you hanging out with that young dude?"

"That young brother got more sense than most of you sad old suckers," I-Ron shot back. I liked that he thought that, even if it wasn't always completely true.

Since I was small compared to the older guys I hung out with, to me it made "sense" to get a gun when I was eleven. It was a nickel-plated Colt .25 that made a loud-ass noise when you fired it. We were partying in all the boroughs, and sometimes things got a little crazy. Being able to pull it out could defuse a lot of situations. I loved carrying it. When I had it, I felt like I wanted to dare people to mess with me. It made me feel strong and tough and impenetrable. Nothing could stop me. No one could hurt me. Just having it in my pocket made me feel like I could take on the world. Having it was like having freedom because I could go wherever I wanted and not worry about a thing. When I had that iron on my hip, I felt like I could dare anyone to say something. I could walk through any part of the hood and move through any group of guys and not worry. Holding a gun put an *S* on my chest. It made me feel like Superman.

One night, back at home in my room, I slipped the gun under my pillow and went outside for a minute. When I came back, my father was sitting on my bed. An electric shock ran right through me.

"What's wrong? What are you looking for?"

"I ain't looking for nothing. Already found what I was looking for." He picked up my pillow to reveal the gun.

My heart tried to bounce out my chest.

"What the hell is this?"

"It don't even work." I was too scared of him to be honest.

"I don't know what you doing out there, but whatever it is,

you better be smart about it." He looked at the gun. "This shit is so dusty, when you pull the trigger all it's going to do is backfire.

About a month later, I went to get a soda at a store called Pete's with the Colt .22 in my back pocket. I had on my burgundy denim Lee suit, and the gun always poked out just a little bit. Of course I was in line when two cops stepped up behind me. I started bending my knees so the gun would stay as far down in my pocket as possible, but that attracted their attention, and suddenly the cops got real quiet. I could feel them standing there behind me, looking down at me. I wondered if they could see the little end poking out or, if not, they at least recognized the imprint of the gun. I looked behind the counter at Pete, the store's owner and my father's friend. He always watched out for me like I was one of his own. He could tell something was wrong from the look on my face and the cops standing right behind me, staring down at me, looking for an excuse.

"Li'l Griff, how's your dad doin'?" Pete asked. "Tell him to come see me. I ain't seen him in a while."

He was telling the cops that I had a dad who was cool so I was not one to worry about. I thought it might've thrown them off. I paid for my soda and walked out. A second later the cops were walking out, looking my way. I went onto the path into Wyandanch Park as the cops jumped in their car and whipped around. It looked like they were gonna drive over to the other side of the path and try to catch me coming out. The moment I was out of their sight I pulled out the gun, thinking, *Gotta get rid of these bullets*. Nervous, heart pounding, hands shaking, I pulled out the clip. A bullet was stuck in the chamber. I panicked—had to move fast. I tried to push the clip back into the gun. Rushing, I shoved it too hard. *Boom!* It was loud. I was sure the cops had heard that. Then I started feeling dizzy. I put my hand in my pocket, and it felt like a big knot was on the inside of my thigh. There was a lot of blood. I had shot myself.

My leg started stinging badly. I sat down on a bench, sweating like crazy. I watched it swell up like a balloon taking in air. I could feel the bullet in my thigh, lying there under my skin. My leg kept swelling until I couldn't feel it anymore. *I'm gonna lose my leg. They're gonna cut it off!* I was freaking out. Then my new girlfriend's sister drove by with her boyfriend. They saw I wasn't doing too well, and they helped me into their car and drove me home. The whole drive I was playing it cool, just looking out the window and acting like my leg wasn't killing me. I tried to keep from spilling blood in their car because I didn't want them to go tell my new girlfriend that I'd shot myself. But I was fading in and out of consciousness.

Somehow I was able to stagger into my house. Moms was on the phone, talking to my aunt, in the middle of a heavy conversation. She did not believe in kids interrupting adults.

"Ma, I gotta talk to you."

"Can't you see I'm talking?"

I was sweaty, dizzy, and bleeding. The room was spinning. "Ma, I gotta . . ."

"Hold on, boy. Wait a minute."

I was bleeding to death and Moms had me on hold. Finally I said, "Ma, I been shot!"

She dropped the phone. "What you mean you been shot?" She laid me down on the couch and pulled down my pants. She saw the holes and the blood and the whole mess. "What happened?"

"Shot myself." The bullet had hit me in the groin and was

lodged in my thigh. At that point I was so delirious I thought it was all kinda funny. She didn't. The ambulance came in minutes.

I was in a hospital bed when two cops walked in—the same two cops who had been behind me in Pete's. I just knew they had come to arrest me.

"So what happened to you?"

"I don't know," I said. "I heard gunshots and then my pants was wet. I thought I pissed on myself."

"Did you see who shot you?"

They didn't recognize me from the store. They weren't going to arrest me. I'd escaped. Then my father arrived. Pops looked at me and shook his head in this way that all my brothers and sisters know means *I told you so.*

As soon as I got well, I was back to partying with I-Ron. Ain't nothing changed. We rolled out to a party in Bay Shore, where we didn't know anybody. Got into an argument with some dudes who lived there, and then I-Ron punched one of the dudes in the face and knocked him out. After that, chaos.

I looked up and saw a bunch of glass beer bottles flying toward me. They hit me dead in the face. I fell down, sprang up, and saw these guys coming at me. I was in a fight with two dudes, and that night I didn't have my gun. I saw I-Ron running to his red van to get his weapon out of the glove box. The van had a little triangle window in front of the main window and he was trying to break it, but there were dudes attacking him. He had to kick someone dead in the face to keep them dudes back. Finally I-Ron broke the window with his elbow, reached in, and pulled out a little sawed-off shotgun. When these seemingly fearless guys saw it, they took off running. Ron fired into the air and then everything was quiet. Since they were gone, we stayed at the party.

I said, "Who were those dudes?"

Turns out they were a gang. We found out where they hung out and drove to their block. They saw us coming in a memorable red van and called the cops. Immediately there were sirens and lights flashing everywhere.

A cop pointed his gun at me and ordered me out. "Put your fucking hands on the car or I'll blow your brains out!"

I said, "You ain't blowing nobody's brains out!"

He took his stick and whacked me on the crown of my head with everything he had. I crumpled to the ground. To this day, I can feel the spot on the top of my skull where he hit me.

When I got to jail, they refused to believe I was twelve. But I had no ID because I was twelve. They thought I just looked young, called me "Babyface Griffin" and locked me up with adults. I spent the night in the pen, sleeping on a bench surrounded by grown men, keeping one eye open. I didn't let anyone know I was scared.

I woke up to a voice yelling, "Where the hell is my son?" My pops had come to save me even though he was mad as hell. I knew it was better to be with him than to be in jail, but then again, the ride to jail had been nicer than the ride home. Mom dug into me the whole way about how I was ruining my life, barely stopping to breathe as she berated me and dogged me and added new punishments every five minutes. I couldn't go outside for, like, two years. I couldn't do anything fun for three. I had to feed the dogs and take out the trash and do the dishes and . . .

When we got home, Moms got out and stormed into the house. Pops let her walk in by herself.

He said, "You're at the point where you're really jeopardizing your life. If you get caught with another gun, you could go away for a long time." He stopped. "Look, if you want to shoot guns so bad, I'll send your ass to where you can shoot guns all day."

"Where?"

"The army."

"I'm too young for the army."

"I'm talking about military school. The army for boys."

It was really tense in the house for months. I was vacuuming, dishwashing, toilet cleaning, gutter scrubbing—everything. I felt like I was in a prison work camp. But I did my work with a smile because I was trying to put things at a better temperature with Moms and Pops. I respected them—there was no talking back in my house. I hated letting them down. But I couldn't stop carrying. I craved the adrenaline of the gun. When I was out there with that thing on my waist, I felt gigantic. Years later, when I began to think of the importance of having an alter ego in hip-hop, it brought to mind that Colt .22: having an alter ego as a rapper is like having a gun on you.

FIRST LOVES

She was working behind the register at a store called Red's Discount, and she was wearing a really pretty yellow dress. I'd seen Felicia Everette around before. I was in junior high school and thought of myself as a player, talking to a lot of girls, but when I walked past that store on Easter and saw her through the window, I just had to talk to her. I was twelve and she was eleven, and Wyandanch was small enough that she and I already knew each other a little, but I hadn't thought of her in that way until I saw her in that dress. I went in and asked her for her number.

"Don't you already have a girlfriend?" she asked.

I said no.

She didn't buy it. "If you want to call me, you can look me up."

I already knew that her last name was Everette and her family lived on 29th Street, so I looked through the phone book and found her number in a few seconds.

"Hello, can I speak to Felicia?"

When she realized it was me, she was impressed. Her whole tone changed and suddenly got all flirty.

"How'd you get my number?"

"You said, 'Look me up.'"

We talked for a while and then her sister jumped on the phone.

"Yo, are you serious with my little sister? You better not be playing with her!"

That definitely affected me. It made me take her more seriously when I knew that her family was worried about her and standing behind her. But her father was another story.

After a few weeks of hanging out around school, Felicia said that I should stop by the house. I'd been hoping for that. I wanted her to become my girlfriend. When I walked up the street to her house, I thought I was big and bad. Then I ran into my man Carlos.

"Yo, Lil Griff, what are you doing over here, man?"

"I'm going to Felicia's house!"

"Yo, man, good luck. Her pops be answering the door with a shotgun!"

"What's he gonna do? Shoot me for knocking on the door?" We laughed, but just thinking of him holding a gun made me turn around and go back to my hood. I had to come correct.

I got a fresh haircut and asked I-Ron to let me borrow his car—a beautiful black Barracuda. I could drive even though I was so small it was tricky to see over the wheel and reach the brakes at the same time. I could power-brake too—just step on the brakes and the gas at the same time so the back tires spin hard on the pavement. That sends smoke from the tires everywhere. I-Ron had taught me.

I drove the Barracuda over to Felicia's house, and you couldn't have convinced me that I wasn't the man. I had a hot car, and I was going to see a pretty girl. I pulled up into the driveway. The grass in front of her house looked perfect. Her dad took care of all the fields for the school. So of course the grass at his house was immaculate.

I knocked on the door. Her dad opened up. He had a shotgun hanging down by his leg, and he was not looking at me but past me. Suddenly I felt tiny.

He didn't say anything, which left a heavy, awkward silence between us. It was probably four seconds, but it felt like ten minutes.

Finally I said, "Mr. Everette, is Felicia here?"

He let that awkward silence settle back in. After a while, he responded coldly with a solitary word. "Yeah." He was still looking past me.

"Could I speak to her?"

He just looked off into the distance. I felt like a bug.

"No."

"Mr. Everette, um, I can't speak to her?"

"No." This time he had some attitude in his voice, like *Boy, you should've heard me the first time.*

I looked at him like *Okay, bet.* I turned and walked across his immaculate grass in my boots. When I hopped into the Barracuda, he was glaring at me. I looked him in the eyes, revved the engine, and started power-braking right in front of his crib, smoking up the whole area, then I let go of the brake. The Barracuda screeched, and I jerked off out of the driveway and into the street.

When I got back home, Mom asked, "Is everything all right? Your girlfriend called here, like, five times."

I went to the phone.

"Why did you do that?" Felicia said, pissed. "My father's so mad!" Then her tone changed. "But my sisters say they love you." They were excited because after years of Mr. Bennett chasing all the boys away, finally somebody had stood up to him. They had stood by Felicia when she talked it out with her dad. He said I could never be in their house. Felicia said, "If he can't come here, then I'll see him out in the street." Her dad couldn't have that. They argued for a while, but he couldn't face down all of his daughters at once. Finally I was approved. "If you like him that much, then I'll let that boy come over here." Felicia later shared his terms: "But make sure his ass is out by six. And tell him to never, ever touch my lawn."

Next thing you know, I was hanging out at her house and she was becoming my girlfriend. Felicia was smart and really special. There was something about her that made me say, *I've gotta show her that I'm worthy of her.* She tried to help me—she told me to stop ditching school and stop smoking so much weed. She got mad when I didn't do my homework. Then she told me I should stop carrying guns. I couldn't imagine that. But she truly was my better half.

■ ■ ■

Rap was underground music made for the hood by the hood. It lived in the park parties and in the graffiti people wrote on the walls. It was also present in the style of dress created by people who blended basic affordable clothes, like Lee jeans, tracksuits, and Puma and Adidas sneakers, with pricey Kangol hats, Gazelle sunglasses, and sheepskin coats. Rap also lived in the cassette tapes the youth listened to, dubbed and passed on, that captured the sound and style of groups like the Cold Crush Brothers, the

Fantastic Five, and the Treacherous Three. They were groups of three or four or five MCs who worked together on routines— that's what they called them. They'd rhyme short, witty bits of words and finish each other sentences and have little flashy moves to go with it.

One of my favorite MCs was Grandmaster Caz from the Cold Crush Brothers. Caz had skill and flair, but his wittiness and his humor blew me away. One of my favorite Caz rhymes was "Yvette," about him having a quickie with a girl who's not his. He said, "I was tearing shit up about a quarter to three. / She said, "Caz, somebody's coming." / I said, "Yeah, me." I was never the joke-around type. But Caz reminded me to loosen up a bit on the mic, that it's okay to make jokes.

Cassette tape recordings of Caz and the rest weren't easy to get. You couldn't just go to a store. They were passed around, dubbed, and shared among people who loved the music. Every time I got one, I clung to it like it was gold. It'd be a grainy, amateur record- ing that someone had made with a little tape recorder at a live show, but I could hear the MCs rapping and the crowd cheering or booing. I would close my eyes and feel what it was like to be there.

One day during a party in Wyandanch Park this kid stepped up to the mic. He worked in his father's bakery on Straight Path so everyone called him Doughboy. When he got a break on his shift, he would run over to the park and get on the mic still dressed all in white, with a baker's bib on. He spat a crazy flow of rhymes that bodied the party. He was amazing. The way he rhymed made everybody stop and listen. I wanted to do that. But DJs were not letting me get on the mic in the park.

A lot of DJs dissed me. One in particular was named Pleasure.

He was a top local DJ who had humongous, expensive speakers, and he put them in a garbage can to get an echo. The sound was dope. At one party he started playing one of my favorite songs, "Yes, You Can Can" by the Pointer Sisters.

I said, "Yo, I gotta get on the mic. That's my song! Let me rap to that." I had that feeling. I was gonna kill it.

"Beat it, kid," Pleasure said.

He gave me the back of his hand. Really pissed me off. I wandered over by one of his speakers and waited for him to be distracted. When a fight broke out and he was staring the other way, I put my foot into the garbage can and stomped deep into the middle of his speaker. That's what I would later talk about on "Microphone Fiend," when I would say, "Kick a hole in the speaker, pull the plug, then I jet!" I had to do it—I felt like I was kicking back at all the DJs who ever told me no.

In the late 1970s, Cool Breeze was one of the hottest DJs in Wyandanch, and he had the biggest sound system on Long Island. I knew Cool Breeze because my sister used to date his brother. It wasn't nothing for me to go over to his house and DJ on his equipment. He taught me some DJ techniques, but then I asked him to let me rhyme.

"Stop playing. You're too young," he said.

But his homeboy let me rhyme for him. "Li'l Pop Griffin is nice on the mic," he told Breeze.

■ ■ ■

One day in 1979 my brother's friend DJ Maniack came by with a vinyl copy of this new record, "King Tim III" by the Fatback Band. They were a funk band who'd heard that some of their songs were being spun by Herc, and they went to one of his parties. Because of Herc, they added radio DJ Tim Washington to their live set and put out a song with him rapping as a B side. It was the first commercially released rap song ever. I couldn't believe that someone had rapped on a record that had been recorded in a studio. I could hear every word and every vocal inflection. I made Maniack play it seven times in a row.

A few weeks later, "Rapper's Delight" by the Sugarhill Gang came out. To me it was a silly song. I preferred the serious side of rap. When you were rapping, you didn't need to be smiling and cheesing and hamming it up like R&B cats did. Hip-hop was liberation from all that. "Rapper's Delight" was a happy-go-lucky party record that felt, to me, like a novelty record. Rap was about positivity, but why were they that happy?

Around then my brother Ronnie went on tour with Kurtis Blow and played keyboards in Kurtis's band. Blow was a Harlem rapper with a Jheri curl, gold chains, a Hollywood smile, and a massive hit called "The Breaks," which made him the first solo rap star. Ronnie would be gone for a few weeks, then come back for a few days and tell me about the touring life. It blew me away that my brother actually knew Kurtis Blow.

SCHOOL DAZE

Football came to me so easily, I thought I was born to play. I loved it so much that just putting on the helmet got my heart going. I grew up playing in the street with the big guys in the neighborhood and playing in the Police Athletic League (PAL) intracity competitive football programs from the age of seven. At home, Pops had me and Stevie practice out in the backyard every afternoon, just to make me tougher. Stevie was way older and bigger than me, so once I knew how to deal with him chasing and tackling me, the kids in my grade were like nothing. I'd get out on the field and when guys tried to tackle me, I ran into them. I knocked down a lot of linebackers.

By the time I reached seventh grade, I could throw harder and run faster than everyone else, so the coach made me the quarterback. I was never one of the biggest guys on the team, but I was always the toughest. I was thin and short and all muscle and low to the ground, so I was tricky to catch and hard to knock down. I could blow by people with my quickness. No matter what was happening on the field, I could slow things down and look ahead of the guy in front of me and find a way to get past him.

I made plays when no one thought it was possible. Every time we absolutely needed some yards, they relied on me. I loved the gladiator-like contact and, at the same time, the way the game felt like a high-speed chess match with life-size human pieces in it.

One day we had a home game scheduled, but it was raining as hard as hell. It was a torrential downpour. I thought Noah was about to show up with his ark. I knew the game was canceled, so I went home after school. A little while later, the phone rang.

"Hurry up and get down here!" one of my teammates shouted frantically from the phone. I could hear someone else laughing in the background. I thought they were trying to play a joke on me. Nobody fools me. I hung up on him.

"They're out there joking around, trying to get me to go over to school in the rain when the game is canceled," I told my father.

"Are you sure?"

"Well, I didn't hear from coach, but . . ."

Pops drove the few miles over to school and came right back. "They're up there playing," he said when he walked hurriedly back into the house.

"What?"

"They're halfway through the first quarter."

I threw on my gear as Pops drove me there. When I got to the field, there were two minutes left in the second quarter and we were losing 13–0. I ran to the sideline.

"Coach, I need the key to the locker room so I can get my shoulder pads."

"Griffin, you won't be needing those today!" he barked back at me.

I went and sat on the bench. I hated disappointing him. I hated letting the team down. Worst of all, we were losing because of my stupidity. When halftime came, coach yelled at me the whole walk to the locker room. Once we got inside, he ignored me and talked to the backup quarterback about what we were going to do in the second half.

On the first play, the backup QB lined up under center, then stopped and called a timeout. He walked over to the coach and said, "I ain't playing unless Griff plays."

"Yeah, me too," the running back said.

"I agree. We need him out there, Coach," another player said. "We'll run laps for Griff tomorrow. Just let him play now."

That team was like a family. I loved the guys, and they loved me. So when they stood up for me, I wasn't surprised.

Coach yelled at me in front of everyone, telling me if I pulled something like that again I'd be off the team.

"Coach, it was an accident! You know I always show up to play football!"

"All right, Griffin's back at quarterback. Let's go."

I set myself under center and looked around. Down 13–0, I had to get us sparked right away. It was still raining like crazy. The ground was a muddy swamp. But the energy was boiling inside me. I had one half to erase my mistake and make it up to the team.

First play we called was a quarterback option, but in my mind there was no option. I dropped back and started running around the right side, pretending like I might flick the ball to the running back, but as soon as I saw a little gap, I faked the pass, then burst through the hole. I had two good jukes and made three people miss me. In the open field, I turned on the jets and ran 80 yards for a touchdown. In the fourth quarter, I drove us into the red zone and threw for a short touchdown. We won the game 14–13.

•••

Any time we had band practice in school, I was there early. I was first saxophone, which means I had the leads, the complex melodies, and the solos at school assemblies. When it came to music, I was an A student. I loved it, studied hard, and was a quick learner when it came to new concepts. Everything I learned got soaked right into my soul. I had more musical experience and more knowledge than the other kids, and I felt really free with my saxophone, having picked up quite a bit from my older brothers, so I played with a certain swag.

As a seventh grader, I got picked to enter one of the most exciting events of my young musical life. In the little world of New York high school bands, one of the ultimate achievements is going to the NYSSMA, the New York State School Music Association. Everyone wants to go there, even though it means doing a lot of work. They pick the best musicians in each school and put them in a competition. First, they send a song to your school, and you have two weeks to memorize it. Then, on the day of the competition, they give you another song, and you have to play the song you've been practicing and a song you've never seen before. You get graded on both. I don't remember the songs—it was band music, so maybe it was some of the '60s songs that were popular with high school bands at the time, like Dionne Warwick's "Walk on By" or Classics IV's "Traces"—but I remember I practiced my ass off before the competition. I wanted to win.

On the day of the event, they sent us to one of the big high schools in the area. I watched other kids take their turns, and I saw a lot of talented people, but no one made me feel outclassed, and as more and more kids played, I felt like I was one of the best there. When it was my turn, I stepped up in front of the judges—three professional music teachers with long, serious faces. When I said hello, they didn't smile. I tensed up. It felt like my spine was steel, but I took a breath and closed my eyes and forgot that anyone else was there. I felt myself down in my parents' basement, playing alone. I launched into the song I had prepped, and I felt like I went inside the song. I crushed it. When I finished, the judges had little smiles on their faces. They gave me another song to play, one I'd never seen before, and I played it almost perfectly—I messed up only two notes. I only got a B+, which surprised me because I thought I had played well enough to win. It didn't matter. I walked away certain that in my age group I was one of best musicians around.

. . .

One night in the park, Breeze was DJ'ing and throwing on all these breakbeats, and no one was grabbing the mic to rap. I was sitting there like *Ain't nobody going to rhyme on this?* His friend told him he should let me get on, and he finally said okay. I went up there and did my little thing, a twelve-year-old MC, and I killed it. Breeze said I was dope and he'd let me get on the next time he had a party. Then I convinced some of Breeze's crew and some of my friends to create a group. It was me, my man I-Ron, G-Stro, Snake, and Blade. They were all teenagers, fourteen to seventeen years old. No one cared that I was much younger.

"Let's call it the Love Brothers," one of the guys said. I was down with that. I became Love Brother number four. I gave myself a new MC name: Kid Wizard. It could be shortened to Kid Wiz or the Whiz Kid, so it had some flexibility. It also challenged me to be my best—it was a name I had to live up to. If I called myself Kid Wizard, then I had to sound smart.

All of us MC'ed, but I wrote most of the rhymes. I'd listened to enough tapes that I was pretty good at making up routines where everyone played a part in every verse, and they all had something fly to say every time they touched the mic. I wrote a lot of rhymes on the spot, just hours before we went onstage. We did shows all over town—parks, high schools, rec halls, wherever. The Love Brothers lasted a few years and then faded away, but "Rapper's Delight" ignited a fire that blazed beyond anyone's imagination.

"King Tim III" and "Rapper's Delight" were bright records that were escapist and fun and dance-y, like disco. If hip-hop had followed the lead of those songs, it could've turned into light party music. It didn't because a lot of us followed the lead of a song that came out a little later: "The Message" by Grandmaster Flash and the Furious Five. Flash was a legendary DJ and another one of the fathers of hip-hop. He found five MCs to be in his crew, including Melle Mel, one of the greatest of all time because of his tough, gritty voice and the way the sound of it communicates so much. His pen is so blunt and direct and powerful. "The Message" was Mel's tour de force and the group's biggest record and one of the most important records in hip-hop history because it showed us how to make great songs about our reality. "The Message" showed us there was much more power in making serious records that were painful and honest to a fault. At the end of the song, the guy dies in prison. That was so far away from anything we ever heard on the radio. It was far away from what could be heard in the era of routines. It was a hard look at how bad things were in the hood.

In the first lines of the song, Mel is like a movie camera. "Broken glass everywhere, people pissing on the stairs, you know they just don't care." In the chorus, he kinda spits each word out staccato style, heightening the gravity of it all: "Don't push me 'cause I'm close to the edge. I'm trying not to lose my head." That sort of reality music was what I wanted to do.

． ． ．

By the time, I began high school in 1982, I was known for wearing full-length bombers, Kangol hats, mockneck shirts—all the freshest hip-hop styles. I was fourteen, and I was done with begging my parents and brothers and sisters for money. To keep up my self-image and my reputation, I had to find work. I did a bunch of little jobs—I was a telephone marketer, I cut graph paper at a paper store, I did time in the deli, but I bounced around from job to job quickly because I wanted to get paid but I didn't want a boss. I'd work for, like, two weeks, get my first check, and quit, because having a boss was wack. The first time a boss spoke to me in a funky way, I was looking at the front door.

At one place the first day I got there the boss expected me to know what I was doing. He asked me if I understood what to do. I said, "Not really. It's my first day."

"I didn't ask you if it was your first day," he snapped. "I asked you if you knew how to do this."

I left.

For a little while I worked in Filene's Basement in Queens. I was on the crew that came in after hours and buffed floors with big-ass machines. That was the first job I actually liked. The boss was very hands-off. When we took breaks, the boss would go outside and we'd sit in the back and eat in this little room. One day I went to find out where the boss went. Midway through the break, I left to go to the bathroom, and on my way there, I got lost on purpose. I found him in the jewelry section, easing the latches off the jewelry cases. He had realized that if he could get the latches off, he could just peel a metal piece back, lift the glass up, and reach in and grab the jewelry. He was over there stealing all kinds of stuff.

I slid up beside him.

"Don't say nothing," he said. "Help me lift this glass."

He showed me how I could help, and we lifted the glass off, reached in, and grabbed two chains. He said it was critical to never steal too much because that's when people got caught. The next night when break time came, I was on his heels. Same drill. Before I knew it, I was walking around Wyandanch with a bunch of gold chains and my girl had tennis bracelets, earrings, necklaces—everything. A few nights later, he got caught. It was a night I wasn't there. I dodged that bullet.

My pops saw that I was trying hard to make some money, so he decided to show me how to work smart.

He said, "You ready for a little hustle?"

"Yeah."

"Okay. I got something for you. But you gotta stick with it. If you do, you're gonna see a nice little check down the road."

I was open. Pops took me down to the wholesale store, walked me to the back, and hooked me up with a frankfurter cart so I could cook and sell hot dogs on the street. I thought, *This ain't gonna work.*

He could see me thinking that. He kept saying, "Trust me, man."

He told me the prices I should charge—75 cents for a hot dog, $1.75 for a sausage, 50 cents for a soda. He set me up and went out on the street with me that first day to make sure I knew what I was doing. After that I was on my own, selling franks from my own cart in front of the stores on the strip on Straight Path in front of Red's Discount, where I'd met Felicia.

The cart made me my own boss. I could set up when I wanted. I could leave when I wanted. No one would yell at me. I could be my own man. Every morning I'd just get the cart, clean it, roll it out on the block around 11 a.m., start the fire, put my hot dogs in, and within five minutes, "Yo, let me get two hot dogs, man!" I developed a steady clientele, and soon enough I had Kangols in every color and Adidas shell toes with fat laces and Pumas and Wallabees.

■ ■ ■

My father worked the graveyard shift at the airport. He'd come home in the morning around 7:30 a.m., and even though he'd just finished a full shift, he would drive me to school. I was such a knucklehead by this point that I'd jump out the car, walk into school, pop out a side door, and head over to a friend's crib. Once there, I'd usually smoke weed, spin some records, and make a tape. Outside of music, I wasn't a model student in junior high. I got some As, some Bs, and mostly Cs. I got Cs in Spanish and English and math. Basically, I did well enough to be able to meet the criteria for playing on the football team. If a class was first period, I was definitely getting a C. Either I wasn't there or I was so tired my mind wasn't. Around 11 o'clock I'd go down to the lunchroom and stay for three straight periods, skipping classes just to rhyme with people. I cut class a lot.

One time I flowed out of school and started walking down the street when I felt this car creeping up behind me. If I was walking away from school and I heard a car coming, the last thing I'd do is turn around because then I could get caught. So I looked at the ground, hoping it wasn't my father, but I knew it was. I was walking, but inside I was frozen like when you shine a light on a roach and it doesn't move. He was following me and I knew it and he knew that I knew it and my heart was beating out of my chest, but I refused to turn around and admit defeat. I just kept walking.

He pulled up alongside me. "Get in the car."

I did.

"You don't want to go to school?"

I was quiet.

He said, "Look, if you don't want to go to school, you ain't gotta go to school."

"What?" I didn't know where he was going, but I liked where he'd started. I hated school.

"I'll take you back to school right now and sign you out and you won't have to go no more."

"Okay!" Not going to school was my dream.

"But if you ain't going to school, you gotta join the Job Corps. Today. I'll take you up there right now."

Job Corps is a program that basically identifies high school students sixteen and older who are losing interest in school and want to leapfrog ahead to learning a trade now, rather than finish traditional high school or drop out.

He said, "You ain't gonna be doing nothing. You're gonna be working."

I could've gotten out of school forever. But if I was leaving just to take on a boss, what was I doing?

I said, "Okay, I'll stay in school."

He was good at getting me to do what he wanted without telling me what to do. He was smooth with the way he taught me. He'd lay out the options I had without forcing anything on me. That little power of choice usually led me to the best decision.

He drove me back to school, and from that point on I didn't cut class anymore. Okay, I stopped cutting for a little while. After a couple of weeks, I was back to cutting class all the time. When I actually went to class, I'd sit there thinking, *What good does it do for me to know this?* But my English teacher, Ms. Bonaparte, wouldn't take no for an answer. She was the type who walked the halls looking for kids and telling them to come to her class. One day she caught me by my locker and said, "William, I heard you're into rapping. If you like rhymes and putting words together, you need to be in my class." That got my attention. I stopped by the class, and she gave me a page with forty multisyllabic vocabulary words on one page. I was like, "Yo, Ms. Bonaparte, I love you."

I gobbled up the four- and five-syllable words and kept going to the class looking for words for my rhymes. Then she showed me how writing a book report is like writing a rhyme. They both have characters, a setting, a theme, and the writer has to explain it all to the audience in a way that makes them see why they should care. I started really absorbing every minute of English class. I didn't love it all—I didn't like that Mark Twain character, Huckleberry Finn. I thought he was a little jerk. But I dug Shakespeare. I loved the complexity of his sentences and his dramatic flair with language. His words went halfway around the world just to say the simplest things. I tried putting that into my writing.

SPIRITUALITY

The Mystery
(Who Is God?)

[Hook]

If you can see, if you can solve the mystery
The answer revolves around your history.
So carefully, I drop this degree
Scientifically, and realistically
Who is God?

[Hook]

An eternal blackness, in the midst of the darkest night.
Proteins and minerals exist within specks of light.
Solids, liquids, and gases, and sparks of light within
infinite lengths and widths and depths and heights.
No beginning or ending, the seven dimensions,
enough space for more than a million worlds and inventions.
To travel through time within enough room to be the womb
of the most high's great mind, which he will soon make shine
with intelligent elements in sight that he will gather.

In the realms of relativity electricity struck matter.
Energies explode, he reload and keep releasing
atoms by the millions, until the numbers increasing.
Until it was burning he kept returning itself to the source.
The hotter his thoughts it gave the center more force.
He gave birth to the sun, which would follow his laws,
all caused by his mental intercourse.
Who is God?

[Hook]

He began to explain his craft, the master in the attic.
He dealt with measurements, his language was mathematics.
His theoretical wisdom of the numerical system,
the complete number nine, which means born or existing.
He gave birth to all planets, inorganic and organic,
so you wouldn't take it for granted.
They rotated their own distance around the sun
and fully submit to the existence of one,
and each one was promised everlasting perfection
if each one keeps spinning in the same direction,
to the east and each speak the motion of peace
and harmony and each show devotion and teach.
The universe is to come, the whole world must go according.
Know your galaxies and mirages, and your stars start falling.
So stay in orbit, maintain safe and sound.
Like the planets, your cipher remains perfectly round.

[Hook]

From unconsciousness to consciousness,
by Knowledging his Wisdom his response is this,

an Understanding, which is the best part.

He picked the third planet where new forms of life would start.

He pursued show and prove every move in order.

Back to the source he let off his resources in the water.

Climb his climax, where the climate is at, high degrees.

See he start to breathe deep in the darkest seas.

And the plan is to lay in the clays to form land

and expand, using the same clays to born man.

In his own image our origin begins in the East.

Culture rise to breed, with the Powers of peace.

Deal in Equality nature's policy is to be God.

Build or Destroy positively Born life like Allah.

And each one was given everlasting perfection

if each one keep living in the same direction.

And life was life, and love was love.

We went according by the laws of the worlds above.

They showed us physically, we could reach infinity,

but mentally, through the centuries we lost our identity.

Life started ending, we got trife and started sinning,

lost touch with the beginning, now our ciphers stop spinning.

And what was once easy became confused and hard,

which brings us back to the mystic question, who is God?

Sixty-six trillion years since his face was shown,

when the seventh angel appears, the mystery will be known.

Check Revelations and Genesis, St. Luke and John.

It even tells us we are Gods in the Holy Qur'an

Wisdom, Strength, and Beauty, one of the meanings of God.

G-O-D, you and me, Gomer, Oz, Dabar,

Knowledge, Wisdom, Understanding, Sun, Moon, and Star,

Man, Woman, and Child, and so is Allah.

[Hook]

Bear witness that Allah gave birth to all,
for Allah was all, and therefore, life itself.
And the universe gave birth to man.
The universe was man, and man was the universe.
And the universe was always in existence.
And existence was life.
And life is Allah.
And Allah had no beginning because he is what always was.
Rakim Allah, peace.
Now who is God?

Notes on "The Mystery (Who Is God?)"

This song is about answering the question that a lot of people ask, "Who is God?" I started by posing the question and then presented facts on how the universe and human beings came into existence. I wanted to make people think, but I also wanted to explain my ideology, once and for all. I started sharing small tidbits and jewels in my lyrics after I began deeper study, largely because of my awakening through the teachings of the Five Percent Nation. In the beginning, I was disguising it, being cautious, knowing I was trying to give hip-hop listeners something they were not used to, something they may or may not want at the party, something they may not want on their hip-hop CDs. I would shy away from the lessons, or find ways to disguise it so it sounded cool or familiar. By 1997, when I put out "The Mystery" on *The 18th Letter*, seven years after *Let the Rhythm Hit 'Em* received five mics in *The Source* magazine, I was feeling more as if this was the type of music my audience was coming to expect from me.

I remember the day I wrote this song. At the same time, I barely remember anything about that day before getting that beat. I just remember standing in front of the speakers, hearing it. When I heard that beat, that's when that day started.

I had the concept for "Who Is God?" for a while. I wanted to use it for a couple of previous albums but didn't have the right beat. I finally got the track from my man Shorty, from Brooklyn. I met him through Bill Blass. (Rest in peace, Bill Blass.) Shorty used to make beats and played the song for me one day in the studio. As soon as I heard those strings on that song I knew that was it, right there. The track said, "This is the perfect song to use for 'Who Is God?'" I knew I had my work cut out for me. Could I actually explain the high science, make it entertaining to listen to, and create a song that rhymed at the same time? I had no idea how I wanted to approach it, but I knew I had a lot of information I could speak on.

I remember heading back to the hotel where I was staying with my family and not even knowing if I was going to be able to write that night. A hotel has never been my normal comfort zone for writing. But there was a sense of urgency because we were at the end of the album and only had another week to turn everything in. To be honest, I didn't want to write that night, because my tendency is to pick some complicated challenge of a track. I used to call it putting myself in a hole like, *Damn, Ra, you could have made an easy song. But instead you got this crazy rhyme pattern. You're trying to do the whole sixteen bars rhyming with that one word*, and on and on. At that point in the day, I didn't think I had the patience.

When I got to the hotel, my family was in the living room and kitchen areas of the suite, so I went into the bedroom. The sun was still shining. I played the track again. Listening to it at first, I was a bit anxious, trying to figure out what to say. There wasn't a table in there. I could either lie on the bed, which would have been too comfortable, or sit in this uncomfortable-looking chair. So (I'll never forget this) I sat down on the floor with my back leaning against the bed, pulled my notebook out, and started writing right on the floor.

Sitting there listening for a while, I realized that the track sounded like I was in outer space. *Okay,* I thought. *What better place to start if I'm explaining who God is?* "An eternal blackness, in the midst of the darkest night. / Proteins and minerals exist within specks of light." Once I started there, everything just fell into place and I was able to start spinning it out. It started flowing from one bar to the next. Of course that gave me confidence. I couldn't believe how something that I thought was going to be complicated flowed so well. Even though it wasn't easy, I knew exactly what to say next. There was no tug-of-war. It was like bang, bang, bang. Sometimes I had to think for a minute, but I remember reading it back to myself and saying, "This is coming out perfectly."

As I began getting even more amped, I incorporated more elements, dressing it up. I even referenced the Supreme Mathematics from the Five Percent Nation's lessons—from "knowledge" all the way to "born," which is from number one to number nine, zero being the cipher. I saw that as an extra bonus, something for the gods who know what's up and would instantly realize it: "He's quoting the math through the song." I start with knowledge—"By acknowledging his wisdom his response is this, / an understanding"—and then continued through to the hook.

His theoretical wisdom of the numerical system,
the complete number nine, which means born or existence.
He gave birth to all planets, inorganic and organic,
so you wouldn't take it for granted.
They rotated their own distance around the sun
and fully submit to the existence of one,
and each one was promised everlasting perfection
if each one keeps spinning in the same direction,
to the east and each speak the motion of peace
and harmony and each show devotion and teach.
The universe is to come, the whole world must go according.
Know your galaxies and mirages, stars start falling.
So stay in orbit, maintain safe and sound.
Like the planets, the cipher remains perfectly round.

I had a neighbor on Long Island who followed my music but didn't study Islam. One day after *The 18th Letter* came out, I went home to Long Island. When he saw my car pull into the driveway, he came outside.

"Yo, Ra. I got the new album."

"Word. Yo, good looking out, my dude. What did you think?"

"I love it! Congratulations. Good work," he said excitedly.

"Thanks, G. What's your favorite song?" I asked him.

"'Who is God?'!"

That was surprising. Maybe my fault for stereotyping people and assuming they were not into certain things, but I didn't expect that from him. Really, I didn't expect the song to resonate with anyone except the gods. That was a hugely unexpected plus.

I almost finished the entire song while sitting on the floor writing. One of the things about the process that was the most time-consuming aspect was checking my work to make sure I had all the facts right. I made sure I worded everything properly so that it couldn't be disputed—from the composition of our physical structure and how Earth was born to how the planets were formed. I was able to get everything in. I even squeezed in some extra information at the end from Judaism, Christianity, and Islam to underscore my main point:

When the seventh angel appears, the mystery will be known.
Check Revelations and Genesis, St. Luke and John.
It even tells us we are Gods in the Holy Qur'an.
Wisdom, Strength, and Beauty, one of the meanings of God.
G-O-D, you and me, Gomer, Oz, Dabar,
Knowledge, Wisdom, Understanding, Sun, Moon, and Star,
Man, Woman, and Child, and so is Allah.

Of course some of the more traditional religious believers said I was one of the most blasphemous dudes they ever encountered: "Who do you think you are?" "How are you going to sit here and tell me that you are God and that you can interpret the Qur'an?" These were the type of questions I got from the folks I offended the most. In 2009, "Holy Are U," which is on *The Seventh Seal* album, generated the same and additional responses: "Jesus didn't walk on water? What are you talking about? It's in the Bible," were the type of comments folks made in reference to the lyrics "Walk on water, nah, neither did Jesus. / It's a parable to make followers and readers believers. / From Egypt to Budapest, Rakim is the truest left. / Understand the scriptures like the Minister Louis F."

In the Bible it says Jesus walked across the water, and then Peter went to walk across the water to meet him, but he only got halfway and sank. Basically, the point is that you can't believe in God halfway. That's why I said, "It's a parable to make followers and readers believers." In other words, it's not about Jesus walking across the water. It's about what can happen if you don't fully believe. Being able to put out rhymes like that made me feel that my work was providing a valuable service. For sure, there are some people who will never agree with my view that "man is God," a belief at the core of my ideology, but at least through songs like these they were made aware of different views and different ways of understanding our purpose on this Earth.

BELIEVE IN SOMETHING GREATER THAN YOURSELF

To be a good writer you have to be sensitive to what's going on in the world. This means that you have to learn how to sympathize and relate to what people go through. You also have to communicate that back to them through your work—whether to comfort, to motivate, or to heal. Knowing there is a higher power makes it easier to understand not only how to do that but also your role in the process and your purpose for doing so.

Knowing there is a higher power connects you to something greater than yourself. When you respect something higher than you, it makes you more powerful. But it also makes you more humble. Humility exists between the extremes of knowing you can be better and knowing deep down that you are not the best. Humility reminds you that you are no better than anyone. Even as you strive to be better, there is always room for improvement.

With sympathy and humility, you achieve a more universal effect and your values and creative output evolve. My spiritual beliefs, the scientific and mathematical concepts I've studied, the ideas and philosophical questions that inspire me, have helped shape my journey. This is evidence to me that if you can accept that there is a higher power—even just acknowledge a higher creative power—then you have already taken the first step on the path toward becoming a better artist.

I wasn't born into Islam in a traditional sense. My parents weren't Muslim. They weren't regular churchgoers either, even though the community I grew up in was mostly Christian. During my elementary school years, one of my good friends who lived down the street was the son of a pastor in Brooklyn, and another friend attended church in Deer Park. I would attend with them sporadically, but I never felt a strong enough pull or connection to join a church. I felt more like an outsider, or at best an observer. Still, these experiences gave me a foundation, and helped to create a spiritual curiosity in me that motivated me to pursue my own path to righteousness.

At the end of 1985, a little before my seventeenth birthday, I came into an understanding through the Five Percent Nation of knowledge as the pathway to self-empowerment— what the Five Percenters call "knowledge of self." At that point I didn't have 120 degrees, the lessons—or questions— that Five Percenters read and use to help them develop a greater understanding of themselves, so they can reach knowledge of self. I then was just starting my lessons, but I was able to read them and get the understanding before a lot of people. And from there I started reading the Bible to confirm what I was reading. That led me to read the Qur'an and the Torah. I would refer to the Torah a lot, partly because I was fascinated with Nostradamus. He was the grandson of a high priest who was known to have a deep understanding of biblical text. Some people believe he may have used this understanding to decode the Torah and based his well-known predictions on what was revealed. I was also able to read these texts and read in between the lines to draw an understanding of things that, given my young age then, some thought were over my head. I believed it was a type of gift and that if I could decipher the information, I should find a way to share what I'd learned through my lyrics and songs. When you share knowledge, consistently and unobstrusively, people will start to commend you for it. If you put your ego aside, you realize that helping others achieve understanding is something greater than the act and greater than yourself. Likewise, as you mature intellectually and spiritually, you recognize that maybe you are being guided by a higher power.

I began by studying Clarence 13X Smith through the Five Percent Nation. Next, I studied who came before him (Elijah Muhammad of the Nation of Islam) and who taught him (Fard Muhammad). It made sense to me to trace my roots back in this way. It nurtured a passion already within me for understanding how humans evolved, beginning with the earliest civilizations. Studying made me realize that something was going on that scholars are still unable to explain. It was baffling. It was amazing. It was genius. It was a mystery. It was all this at one time. This took me back to studying ancient Egypt, Mesopotamia, the pyramids and monuments in Egypt and elsewhere. How could we go from there and then wind up here? Why haven't humans continued to intellectually evolve? Why is it so hard to get back to the knowledge people had during that time? How were humans so intelligent then and now we have just mediocre or common-sense intelligence? So much about those ancient structures was impossible to achieve based on what humans knew. There's no proof that the first humans roaming Earth and starting civilization knew geometry. But the monuments were built with geometry. For example, the Great Pyramid of Giza is placed directly in the center of Earth's landmass. How could a human know that and build it exactly at the intersection of the longest line of latitude and the longest line of longitude? So I started asking questions like "Who built this?" "Do these monuments tell us that aliens exist?" Machu Picchu, Chichén Itzá—there's no way humans did this.

Another thing I studied was the golden ratio, a proportion between objects that equals essentially 1.618, and how it affects nearly everything. It's intelligence. It's not a coincidence. Like the measurement from your toes to your belly button is 1.618 times longer than the distance from your belly button to the top of your head. It doesn't matter how tall you are. Spiraling patterns with the same golden ratio are also found in flowers and trees. That's crazy. The surface area of the Great Pyramid divided by the area of its base also equals the golden ratio. This embedded intelligence shows us there's a higher power. Certainly at that point the grass is not boring. Flowers, trees, fruit, the way living things grow—you start to appreciate things a little more. As an MC, this information only helps me express myself better.

I never wrote a rhyme about grass, but learning about the golden ratio gave me a deeper understanding and a deeper love for life.

My studies also led me into religious debates as to whether or not man is God. On one occasion, a handful of Jehovah's Witnesses knocked at Felicia's father's door while I was visiting. Most folks have had this type of experience, believing what you believe and going through an encounter that feels like you are being recruited right on your own doorstep. They asked me if I belonged to a church and what I thought about God and salvation. They went on and on with questions about the good news, salvation, and Armageddon. "But doesn't it also say . . . ?" "Yeah and what about . . . ?" "And doesn't it say that . . . ?" Before long they were trying to shove their views down my throat and make me agree with what they were trying to tell me. Eventually they started asking me about the Bible, which forced me to tell them how I felt.

"Do you read the Bible?" the one doing most of the talking asked.

"Yeah, I read it a little bit."

"Well, what do you believe?"

Thinking, *I'm glad you asked*, I asked them to open their Bibles to Psalms 82:6. "Right here it says we all are Gods." I read aloud, "'I have said Ye all are Gods, Children of the Most High.'"

"Oh no, that's not what it says. That says that Ye are God's Children of the Most High."

"But that doesn't make sense," I insisted.

"What do you mean? It says we all are God's children."

"No, it says, 'Ye all are Gods,' comma, 'Children of the Most High.' The way you are reading it, it would mention God twice. Why would it say, "Ye all are God's children' and then repeat 'Children of the Most High'? Or basically, we are all God's children of God?"

They stood there at the door looking at me. Finally the one who had been the most cavalier broke the awkward silence, saying they're going to have to go and get brother such and such.

"Yeah, go get him," I said.

I was seventeen and already steadfast, facing down grown-ups about what I believed. Sending them scurrying for backup. That experience proved to me that I knew something. Soon I would come to know that 109 passages in the Bible say that man is God.

Over the years, I continued to make these references in my rhymes, and I would often get into debates with Masons, Shriners, and brothers from the Nation of Islam when they heard me rapping about my beliefs.

One time this came in the form of a letter. It wasn't a disrespectful letter. It came from someone at the mosque. Brother Rakim, we appreciate your work. We love what you do, lifting up messages of righteousness for our young people. You are such a valuable asset by always bringing positivity." It was a positive letter, but then there was this: "But we do have a problem with you saying that the Holy Qur'an states that man is God. It doesn't say that."

The letter made me realize that I'd struck a nerve, but I didn't respond to the letter. I just let it go because at this point in my life I hadn't studied the Qur'an in depth. I was a little discouraged by how complicated and consuming it could become, so I started reading other literature that pointed me to several passages in the Qur'an that I felt supported the view that man is God. Even though I believed I was right, I didn't want to misinterpret what I was reading. And I definitely didn't want to misinform anyone. A couple of years after that, with a deeper understanding of how I could approach it, I started trying to read the Qur'an again. This time I navigated it thinking, *Ra, you're gonna have to read this whole Qur'an if that is what it takes to find passages that confirm what you're saying.* After I read more, I felt like I had a better understanding of what I was reading. And this time, my studies led me to a chapter in the Qur'an called "The Greatness of Man."

It's self-explanatory. The chapter speaks on how man was given dominion over the angels. The angels started to ask the Most High questions like "How you going to give man dominion over us? We're the angels!" And the Most High said, "I know what you do not know." What is it he knows that they do not know? How great was man that he gave man dominion over angels? He knew who man was. He knew the greatness of man. He knew that he made us to be gods. When you read the whole chapter and read between the lines, it's evident what he's telling the angels. When I read it, my body was swelling up as I was getting closer and closer to how I felt. This confirmed what I believed and what I had been telling everybody for years: we were made to be Gods.

"Before God created man, the angels had the opportunity to rule the earth, but if they'd succeeded they would've ruled the Universe. Archangel Lucifer has proved to God, that only beings with His mind could be trusted with such a massive responsibility. But the Angels threw up, man was thorns. God created nothing greater than his perfect sons who will develop his character through trials and tests in the physical life. Though angels have enormous power, you as man have access to far more power . . . As your faith allows us to believe in your potential, your potential is greater than the Angels."

It's a beautiful feeling when you can look at something concrete like that, which confirms something that seems far-fetched to others who claim to have studied Islam all of their lives but still refuse to accept what is right before their eyes.

. . .

I found it almost divine the way the Five Percent Nation af-fected the evolution of hip-hop. It was right there for us. It was in our generation. It was our form of music. And at the same time a lot of us had the gift for using words. It was almost easy for a lot of the rappers who were Five Percen-ters because we had come of age already equipped with a language and information intricate to our studies that em-powered us far beyond the average person on the street. And some of the people who didn't have that information felt it was something they needed to know, something they wanted to know. Sometimes they looked up to us just be-cause we knew.

What we studied entailed religion, history, culture, astron-omy, mathematics, words, literature—all of that and more.

So it was right up our alley to want to express ourselves through rapping. We felt we had something to say that was unique to our time.

Much later in my career, in "The 18th Letter (Always and Forever)," I put it this way:

> From the ancient hieroglyphics, to graffiti painted
> pictures,
> I study I know the scriptures, but nowaday ain't it
> vicious.
> Date back, I go beyond, check the holy Qur'an,
> to speeches at the Audubon, now we get our party on.
> So being beneficent, I bless 'em with dialogue.
> They expectin' the next testament, by the God.

What I was saying was that during the previous era of the 1960s and 1970s, during the Civil Rights and Black Power Movements, our leaders—like Malcolm X—communicated to the people through their speeches and political move-ments. Now, in the golden era of hip-hop, we were com-municating through rap music. Hip-hop had become the podium for anybody who had something to say. By the mid '80s and early '90s, the mosque wasn't as big as it had been for young Black men in the '60s and '70s. The focal point had shifted from the mosque to the hood, the street, the park, and the stage—wherever MCs graced the mic. "Date back, I go beyond" means I was here, or the spirit I use to write my rhymes was here, and has been here since the beginning of time. And it goes from that to "the holy Qur'an, to speeches at the Audubon"—the Audubon Ballroom in Washington

Heights, where Malcolm X and a lot of Black political leaders of his time spoke to Harlem audiences. Malcolm's assassination at the Audubon marked the end of an era. But the rappers were the new voices bringing that message across generations and time. Now it was coming through hip-hop, through the party, through our generational music and voices. Times change, but we still find a way to get these lifesaving messages to the people.

NATION OF GODS
AND EARTHS

When I was a kid, my pops had this oil painting that intrigued me. It was an image of Jesus Christ that he'd painted on black velvet. I just remember staring at it all the time. The way the colors popped off that black was striking to me. I was maybe five or six years old, and I used to take it out of the closet where he stored it and stare at it for a while, then put it back. My father knew I was messing with it, but he never said anything at the time. I didn't really know the meaning of the picture, but ironically, the picture had a lot of significance to what I would find myself doing later on my life's journey.

I once met a man on the block who immediately captivated me. "Peace, my brother," the man said. " I'm trying to get back to my oasis." I'd never heard anyone speak like that. I got the sense that he was wise and sincere. He said he needed some money to get on the train to go back to Manhattan. I had about three dollars in my pocket, and because of the way he spoke, I gave him everything I had. Years later, I realized I had been tested by Allah.

I had met a brother with knowledge of self, and my test had been to recognize him.

A few years after that, I met a brother, named Sekwan, who'd just moved into the neighborhood. He had knowledge of self and an inner calm I admired. He let me know that I had to get enlightened and I had to obtain it myself. He put me on the path to righteousness. He showed me the lessons that we Five Percenters call 120 Degrees of Life, which are used to reach knowledge of self. Studying Islam made me more cerebral and more conscious of the underlying meanings of things. It showed me how to read in between the lines of what I saw around me and analyze everything a little deeper. I was immediately attracted to it. I could tell that this was the path. It gave me a sense of who I was and what I should be doing. It became a guide for my life.

I studied the lessons by myself all the time. Most people have someone help them learn the lessons, but I didn't want someone over me like a boss or a father. I wasn't doing this to take on a new leader. I wanted to liberate myself. This, I thought, would help me become my own man, in control of myself and my destiny. I was constructing my true identity.

Because it was hard to work my way through all the lessons by myself, it took a while. The dictionary became my best friend. I had my nose in it every ten seconds to comprehend what I was reading, but the more I read, the more I grew and the more I learned the importance of telling the truth to myself. Islam taught me to have a more honest relationship with myself. Gaining knowledge of self means having a complete understanding of who you are and where you fit in the universe. When I sat and thought deeply about myself, I uncovered that I am a monument builder. I create big, historic things. I'm a person who has knowledge and wisdom.

I'm no better than anyone else—we're all the same. And there's always room for me to improve. This self-understanding led me to believe if I focused my thoughts I could develop my natural abilities into becoming a mathematician or scientist. And this natural inclination could help me to be a better rapper, a means through which I could construct monuments within listener's minds. And in the process, of course, I could be a better person.

Islam made me want to live up to the expectations of being thoughtful and righteous. Islam set me up to become the MC and the independent man I wanted to be. If I hadn't gotten into Islam and acquired knowledge of self, I would've been a guy from the block talking street trash. I would've been part of the problem. Islam pushed me to be more thoughtful about the world and what I was putting into it.

The name Kid Wizard no longer reflected the person I was, so I turned the word "wiz" into a righteous name and I became Wise Intelligence. Once again I had a name I had to live up to. But after a few months, I changed it again. Islam was becoming more and more of a presence on the streets of Wyandanch, and people were adopting some of the practices and exploring some of the teaching though not always converting fully or committing themselves to the faith. My brother Stevie wasn't studying Islam specifically, but he did temporarily assume the name "Hakim." One day, he wrote the name on the sidewalk, and at first, I just liked the way it looked. Later, when I thought about choosing a name, I decided on "Rakim." It's amazing how the universe works because I didn't know what it meant at the time. I just liked the name because it sounded strong and familiar like "Hakim" but was still original. As my teens became my twenties and I learned the history of the name—that in Egyptian religion "Ra" meant

Sun God, and that "Kem" meant Kemet or Egypt, and "Rakim" also meant "the benevolent one" and variations referred to "writer, architect, builder"—it all fueled power into my purpose.

. . .

I'd go into every party in the park and rap. I love the thrill of rocking a crowd when it's like we (the audience and I) are one and I'm getting energy back from it. It's the best high. I lived for the moments when I could get up in front of people and rhyme in the park. Now that I knew I was going to get on and be heard, I was writing differently. I began writing with an image of where the rhymes would be heard and who would hear them, and I thought about what people wanted to hear and the punch lines that would make them yell. The best feeling in the world was making the crowd respond. It was electrifying when I said something and they went nuts, so I was always thinking, *How can I move the crowd?*

That whole summer of 1986 I rapped from ten in the morning to midnight, every day. I was either in my house rapping or in someone's studio rapping or in the park on the mic. No matter where I was, I was thinking about hip-hop and words and rhymes and rhyme patterns. I was making, like, two tapes a day. I wasn't making songs—each tape was ten to fifteen minutes of straight rhyming with no song structure, no hooks, no choruses. I knew nothing about making songs, but I loved writing rhymes and recording and showing off how good I was. When a beat was going and I was rhyming in the pocket and everything was flowing, it was the best thing in the world. My dream was to make a tape and have somebody in the park play it on a big boom box.

At that point I was the best MC in Wyandanch. The more I knew I was going to be rhyming in front of people, the more I looked at what I was writing and why I was writing it. I asked myself what it meant to be a meaningful MC. I asked myself what it meant to be really truthful with myself and my audience. How could I say something that would matter to them? I wanted to be a conscious member of the community, so I had to be thoughtful about how I could serve the community. I took the thoughtfulness and the deep self-inquiry I was learning from Islam and applied it to the way I practiced hip-hop.

I spent a lot of time fighting with myself about the person I wanted to be on the mic. I thought I should include what I was learning from Islam in my rhymes. I was proud, and I wanted everyone to know that I was in the Five Percent Nation. For "Move the Crowd," a song on our first album, I wrote:

> I'm the intelligent wise on the mic, I will rise
> right in front of your eyes 'cause I am a surprise.
> So I'ma let my knowledge be born to a perfection.
> All praises due to Allah and that's a blessing.
> With knowledge of self, there's nothing I can't solve.
> At 360 degrees I revolve.

But there was a deeper wisdom I had learned from Islam that I could impart. I could go deeper than just saying I had knowledge of self. Part of me said, *You gotta share that wisdom. You're obligated to teach what you know.* But another part of me said, *You're not an expert. It's not your place. You don't know the lessons well enough to be decoding them for others. What if you make mistakes?* I decided to split the difference: yes, I had a duty to share my knowledge, but I could blend the essence of the lessons into my rhymes without quoting them verbatim. I should spread the concepts and the values that made up the lessons rather than the specific words. I wasn't going to give it to them easily. I wanted them to work to figure out what I was saying in the same way I had to work to understand the lessons. The same way I had had to decode the stuff my father told me. I later slipped that into "Paid in Full," which was about making money the right way. After saying "I used to be a stick-up kid," I said, "but now I learned to earn 'cause I'm righteous." In the whole song I tried to tell people to do things in a thoughtful, peaceful, conscious way, and in that line I gave my little nod to the gods, letting them know this idea had sprung from what I'd learned from Islam.

But I was nervous that if I kept weaving Islam into the music, people wouldn't get it. Was I trying to plant a tree in concrete? I looked at my rhymes and said to myself, *You're going over their head with that.* I wanted to make them think, but I didn't want to be so far out of their reach that they didn't get it.

That led me to a new quandary. Should I write in a way that let everyone understand me, or should I write rhymes that let people know I was the best and risk going over their heads? A big internal argument about all this ensued for months. I started debating with myself about every word as if each choice were a monumental decision in my career. I became paralyzed and stopped writing for a few weeks. Finally I decided that I wouldn't dumb my lyrics down one iota, because I enjoyed writing rhymes that people couldn't fully understand at first. I loved making complicated puzzles that people had to solve. I liked sending listeners to the dictionary. I wanted to make people think about the rhymes, because if they have to really think about your work, it'll stay with them longer. I wanted them to have to rewind my lyrics. Once that mind-set settled in, I felt free again.

. . .

This newfound sense of freedom as a writer with a clear vision and mission, and of course my visit to Marley Marl's studio and what it would mean in the days ahead, changed the game. When I got to school the next day, I couldn't wait to tell people that I had been at Marley's house last night.

"That's right, Marley. We're on a first-name basis." That's something you brag about.

I wasn't recording songs at Marley's house for the thrill of it. I loved the respect it got me in the hood. I was now someone who recorded songs at Marley's. I didn't think of it as work or a step toward becoming a professional. It was a serious hobby, but I didn't consider that it could be a big part of my future. Eric was much more business-minded. After we made those two songs, he wasn't thinking anymore about making an album with lots of MCs. He was determined to make one with only me.

At that point Eric was staying in Harlem with his mom, and he found out there was a record label a few blocks from his mother's place called Zakia Records. He had learned about Zakia by reading the credits on a record they'd put out. Eric went over there with a tape of our two songs and introduced himself. The boss wasn't there, but he met Agnes, the receptionist, a white lady who said she used to work at Sugar Hill Records and understood rap. Sugar Hill was the original rap label, the one that put out "Rapper's Delight." Eric played our tape for her, and she loved it. She told Eric to come back the next day and meet Robert Hill, the head of Zakia Records. The following day they sat down.

"I don't know music that much, but Agnes said she loved it, so let's do something," Robert told Eric.

Zakia gave us a check that said "Paid in full."

" 'Paid in full.' That's gonna be the name of the album," Eric said to me.

"That sounds dope," I agreed.

Zakia put out a single—"Eric B. Is President" with the B side "My Melody."

A few weeks later I was walking home and I heard "Eric B. Is President" playing out of a car parked near Straight Path. This random dude was sitting in a car, window open, blasting my song. I was like *How could he have that?*

I walked over and said real nasty, "Yo, my man, who's car is this?"

He looked at me like I was the craziest stranger he'd ever seen. I was eighteen and he was about thirty.

"Yo, that's my song on that tape in there, so whoever owns this car stole my tape!"

He looked at me like *What are you talking about?*

"Isn't that a tape?" I asked.

"It's the radio."

I zoned out, backed up, but kept listening as my voice flowed out of his car. It was surreal to hear my song on the radio. I practically floated home. I couldn't wait to tell everyone I was on the radio! But when I got to the house, my parents were asleep. I sat on the couch and turned on the TV with the news bubbling inside me, dying to get out.

The next morning when I walked into school, everything

had changed. Everyone had heard my songs. Now the buzz was infinitely beyond my previous news, that I had been at Marley Marl's studio. They were all talking about me like I'd made it. And I had, because that was all I'd ever wanted from rap: I got love in the streets, love on the radio, and even more love at home.

When I got home, Mom said, "I heard your record got played on the radio!" She was beaming. Her pride was all the encouragement I needed to get up and go harder.

Our two songs got played on the radio a lot. Marley played them on his show on WBLS, and DJ Red Alert played them on his show on KISS-FM, but it was really a car record. People taped it off the radio, so every ride in the hood was blasting "Eric B. Is President" and "My Melody."

Eric knew all the radio DJs in the tristate area because he'd been out promoting WBLS. Now he took our record to all the DJs he knew and got them to play it. I heard it was on radio stations in Philly, Virginia, DC, and North Carolina. Our name was spreading fast. Zakia gave each of us $17,000 in cash to keep us happy and in close proximity. The company president, Robert Hill, just handed us stacks of hundreds. I stuffed it in my pockets and went straight to the store and bought a blue, red, and white Suzuki 125 motorbike. Suddenly MC'ing looked like a great job. I had to be honest with myself about football—I loved it and I was great at it, but I was a lot shorter than most NFL QBs. Plus, rap had just bought me a motorbike. Rap was no longer a hobby.

■ ■ ■

I started paying close attention to every word or phrase that caught my ear. My mind looked at each word like a scientist examining an atom, considering it from every angle, seeing what I could get out of it. My process became much more complicated. If I was trying to write and the word "Mesopotamia" came up, first I'd try to see what words rhymed with it. Then I'd come up with concepts related to Mesopotamia and I'd start researching those, which led me to other words, like maybe "pyramid." I'd dissect that and uncover all of its meanings and then select words that rhymed with it until another word popped out, and so on. I could easily go through forty or fifty words, just to write one verse.

I started doing more research and more reading, just trying to take in as much knowledge as possible. I was doing anything I could think of to make myself a better artist and a better writer. I started applying myself in all my classes. I paid attention in social studies with Ms. Goldstein and in science and in algebra. I was hungry for any sort of knowledge I could get.

I listened more closely to the jazz I loved. I felt like Dizzy Gillespie was who I'd be like if I was in the jazz world. He was very cerebral and thoughtful. He showed me that I had to expand my knowledge and become smarter in order to take my music to the next level. I had to try to know everything.

Then I watched a documentary on the genius pianist Thelonious Monk and started trying to re-create his sounds and rhythms with my rhymes and flows.

Ronnie and I also watched Miles Davis perform on TV. Miles got up onstage and started playing with his back to the audience. Ronnie had played with Miles. He said Miles was saying, "Kiss my ass." I wanted to be like that.

I started listening to legendary saxophonist John Coltrane's *My Favorite Things* really closely, and when I got to the part where he plays two notes at once, I completely bugged out. I was dumbfounded because you can't play two notes at the same time. I know how to play the sax and I can tell you that it was impossible. But I couldn't deny what I heard. He defied gravity in the same way I remembered Bruce Lee had physically— but Coltrane did it musically. I saw that being the best meant imagining the impossible and then doing it. I couldn't do that with a horn, but I could do that with a mic. I started thinking about my flows and asking myself, *What would Coltrane do?* He became my musical North Star. Coltrane wouldn't stay within the limitations of fours bars, he'd play past the end of the bar, so I tried to write lines that didn't stop at the end of the bar. From his example, I wrote lines like this in "Move the Crowd": "Standing by the speaker, suddenly I had this / fever. Was it me or either summer madness." When I said "this" and took a pause, the listener's mind would fill with anticipation and a little tension because I'd ended the line without concluding the thought. Before me, MCs finished the thought at the end of a line. Coltrane showed me another way.

When I sat down to write my third song, "I Know You Got Soul," I had the sample from Bobby Byrd's "I Know You Got Soul" all looped up, and I was thinking a lot about the Godfather of Soul. I always believed that James Brown was the first rapper. The way he talked on his records with all that attitude and ego shaped the way a lot of performers approached the mic. The way he groaned and screamed and grunted showed me how to use every part of my voice to make myself stand out on a record. He showed me that I could communicate without using words. Those instinctive guttural sounds can really get under people's skin. I didn't understand half of what James was saying. It sounded so good, I'd listen anyway, which made me think it was okay if every person in the audience didn't totally understand everything I said, as long as those people were moved by the music and the rhythm.

I loved James so much I really wanted him to hear my record one day and be proud. I always thought that when he talked about "soul" it meant a lot, like the essence of your humanity, the spirit inside you that makes you who you are. I tried to keep the spirit of the original record alive by the way I rhymed on mine. That was my nod to the way James Brown vocalized.

I wrote "I start to think and think I sink / into the paper like I was ink. / When I'm writing I'm trapped in between the lines. / I escape when I finish the rhyme" because when I was creating rhymes I would stare at the paper and try to put words in between the lines and try to put my real true self onto the paper, and I couldn't get outside those lines, away from the page, until I was done writing. Once I started, I was so locked in that I couldn't even move until I finished.

STRONG ISLAND
TO LATIN QUARTER

We did our first show at a club on Long Island. We performed "Eric B. Is President," "My Melody," and a freestyle. Three songs for $1,500. We did a few more shows before Eric booked us at the legendary Latin Quarter, the most famous, most notorious, and most prestigious rap club in the city.

The Latin Quarter was in Manhattan in Times Square at 200 West 48th Street, between Seventh Avenue and Broadway. Back in the day, this was the club known as the Cotton Club South. Milton Berle, Frank Sinatra, Sammy Davis Jr., and the Nicholas Brothers had all performed there. By 1986, it was a burlesque club during the week. But Friday and Saturday nights hip-hop took over, and everyone who was anyone in the hip-hop game performed there, or DJ'ed there, or went there to hang. Overnight it became the center of the rap universe.

The host and stage manager was Paradise Gray, who a few years later would form part of the rap group X-Clan. Paradise had a knack for getting industry reps in the room—not A&Rs, actual label heads from companies like Profile and Tuff City Records, who showed up every night. A lot of careers were made and ended on that stage. Label owners like Tom Silverman and Monica Lynch (Tommy Boy Records), Fred Maneo (Select Records), and of course Russell Simmons (Def Jam Recordings) were regularly in the crowd. The saying associated with Latin Quarter was that you could perform on Friday and have a record deal by Monday.

The house DJs were Red Alert and Chuck Chillout, the hottest two turntablists in New York City. Their radio shows reached as far north as Connecticut and as far south as Philly. So people came in from Connecticut, Long Island, New Jersey, and of course the illest people from each of the five boroughs showed up. The club's location made it a bit of a neutral territory but there was a lot of tension—violence, robberies, and stabbings. Paradise had a vision for the Latin Quarter as a hip-hop dance club, so people came there to dance to hip-hop. Paradise even had his own house dancing crews, not break-dancers but hip-hop freestyle dancers: the IOUs and the JACs. Before the Latin Quarter, hip-hop acts traveled with a DJ, a rapper, and a hype man. After the Latin Quarter, folks added dancers to the performance.

All of these dynamics earned the Latin Quarter its reputation as the hardest place to perform. It was one of those places where you couldn't come in with nothing but your A game. You had to be one hundred percent on point.

The day before I was hitting the stage, I thought a lot about my aunt Ruth Brown, the famous R&B singer, who had five number-one hits in the 1950s and won a Tony for Best Actress in the '80s. She wasn't really my aunt. She was my parents' close friend. Moms used to drop me off at her house when I was little, and I'd sit and watch her get ready to perform. She put everything she had into every show. The work would start hours before she hit the stage, when she'd pull out her clothes and use clothing glue to put glitter all over her stuff until she looked like she belonged in the Supremes. She spent the entire day getting ready for her shows. It was like she had only one thing to do that whole day. That's a little something I took from her and have never changed—show day is show day. I have my routine pretty much set from the time I'm supposed to hit the stage counting backwards to the time I wake up.

On the day of the Latin Quarter show, I spent the complete day preparing. I didn't drink or smoke. I chose my outfit early. I managed my mood. I stayed focused all day long and acted like I had just one thing to do that day. I thought one million times about the three songs I was going to do. I had learned from Aunt Ruth that to be good onstage I had to be myself while knowing that I was being watched by a lot of people. I focused on what it'd be like to have everyone staring at me. The tension kept my back tight all day long.

When Paradise Gray and Red Alert introduced Eric and me, although the place was said to hold only six hundred, it looked like it must've been eight hundred to a thousand people there, wall to wall. The stage was like fifteen feet high, so the crowd had to look straight up at me.

I hit the stage that night imagining that I had the rock-hard stature of a big-time football player. The crowd saw me, and half of them cheered. Those cheers sent a jolt of energy through my body. I was ready to rock. We did "My Melody" first, and I remember seeing people bob their heads to it, but nobody was dancing. I was like *Damn, do I have to do cartwheels to get them into me?* As soon as we threw on the beat for "Eric B. Is President" and even before

I said a word, the IOU dancers and the JAC dancers rushed to the floor. I started rhyming and the whole building roared. Now they were mine. In that song the sample says "Clap your hands," but there was a heavy echo on that line, and people thought it said "Wop your head." The wop was a huge dance back then where you'd rock your head and arms from side to side to the beat. As I moved around the stage, I saw everyone in the crowd doing the wop. The crowd was dancing so hard I looked down at them, thinking, *This place is on fire right now!* I'd conquered one of the biggest stages in all of rap. I felt unstoppable.

After that, Eric and I did shows at Union Square and the Rooftop, two major venues for rap back then, and a couple of spots in New Jersey. At one club date, I met one of my favorite rappers of all time, Kool Moe Dee. I'd learned a lot about MC'ing by listening to his smooth flows and his wittiness and his deep, gravelly voice. His rhymes showed me how to grab someone's attention. Everything Moe said was dope, and that night Kool Moe Dee said he really liked my records. He said my work felt sincere. That meant a lot coming from a great MC.

A month later, in a club, I ran into Marley Marl and Shan. I hadn't seen them since we were at Marley's house.

Marley grabbed me and said, "I see what you were doing back at the studio." Shan was right beside him.

"We get it now!" they both said together, smiling at me with real love and affection.

■ ■ ■

At the time when Eric and me were doing our thing, getting our first songs on the radio and finishing *Paid in Full*, a new era of hip-hop was blossoming. At established record labels and start-ups, interest was piqued for ways to cash in on the still relatively new musical art form, especially following the growing success of artists like Run-DMC, LL Cool J, UTFO, Salt-N-Pepa, Boogie Down Productions, Kool Moe Dee, MC Lyte, Roxanne Shante, the Beastie Boys, and others being hailed as a new school of hip-hop evolving beyond the pioneers. Likewise, on my native Long Island a world of hip-hop all its own was germinating around us. It encompassed a good deal of the range of diversity and creativity that would come to define the Golden Era.

If you drew a straight line from west to east for twenty-four miles between a string of Long Island towns and hamlets starting with Roosevelt to Amityville to Wyandanch to Brentwood along the Southern State Parkway, and you continued that line for fifteen miles on the Long Island Expressway (locally referred to as the LIE) to arrive at Brookhaven, you would have a pretty good roundup of the hometowns of the artists who contributed to the range of sound that made up the Golden Era of hip-hop.

Biz Markie hailed from the farthest east, Brookhaven. The legendary, innovative beat-box master had a string of hits as early as 1986 ("Make the Music with Your Mouth, Biz," "Vapors," and "Nobody Beats the Biz," followed by albums in 1988 and 1989). Beyond his beat-boxing, Biz was known for his playful party music. Afrika Bambaataa had described the core tenets of hip-hop as "peace, love, unity, and having fun," and Biz's music was true to those roots.

Chuck D and much of the Public Enemy crew, including Flavor Flav and Professor Griff, were from Roosevelt, the farthest west. Their first albums came out in 1987 (*Yo! Bum Rush the Show*) and 1988 (*It Takes a Nation of Millions to Hold Us Back*) and were known for their political content, which many came to classify as "conscious rap" since the content extended the political messages of the Black Power Movement of the '6os and '7os and lifted up Nation of Islam minister Louis Farrakhan. Often my own lyrics were grouped in with this category, as those of us who connected in any way with Islam were often lumped together. Chuck D was a little older than many of us and had already graduated from Adelphi University and was working as a DJ at a local radio station when Public Enemy came together.

A mere six miles from Wyandanch was Amityville, the birthplace of De La Soul, which formed in 1987 and whose debut album would come in 1989, *3 Feet High and Rising*. Posdnuos, Trugoy, and Maseo had met in high school. Playful but not as comedic as Biz Markie, conscious but not as hardcore political as Public Enemy, they helped carve out a socially conscious brand of hip-hop that was deemed "positive" rap by critics who contrasted their approach to the more gritty street sound.

My Long Island contemporaries were rounded out by EPMD (Erick Sermon and Parrish Smith), artists who used their actual names as their stage name rather than monikers. The members of EPMD grew up about eight miles away from me in neighboring Brentwood. They combined party style with a smooth, laid-back flow (a smoothness that irked me because it reminded me too much of my own signature style). One of their songs is a classic ode to the sentiment of the times for many artists seeking a record deal: "Please Listen to My Demo."

Most of these artists would go gold within four to six months after their songs were released before the benchmark for success shifted to platinum by 1988. Of course sales were both bragging rights and a mark of business acumen, but there were other achievements and accolades that become equally if not more important. Eric B. and I were among a handful of artists who received the coveted "Five Mic" album review in *The Source* magazine, which in those days was the highest honor a rapper could receive—to some, more sought after and career defining than a Grammy. Pretty soon De La Soul had "Five Mics" as well, and years later Public Enemy would go on to be inducted into the Rock and Roll Hall of Fame.

The range of major hop-hop artists that Long Island produced reflected the geographical and class diversity of Blacks in the mid to late 1980s. It also reflected the diversity of hip-hop, which had not yet become so heavily melded to the gangsta persona. You could still be perceived as middle class, working class, or college bound or college educated doing hip-hop during that transitional period. The hyper-policing culture alongside the crack cocaine explosion that produced the prison boom was just hitting its stride. Likewise, hip-hop was still being erroneously defined by mainstream media outlets as a strictly NYC phenomenon, despite the emergence of groups like the Geto Boys from Houston, DJ Jazzy Jeff and the Fresh Prince from Philadelphia, Too Short and Digital Underground from the Bay Area, 2 Live Crew from Miami, and of course the various crews from Long Island. N.W.A's emergence would change that forever.

• • •

One of the things that made Eric and I different from a lot of hip-hop groups or acts of any genre is the incredibly short time span that elapsed from meeting each other to having a hit song, a record deal, a major tour, and, most importantly, a recognized brand that indefinitely linked us together. We weren't family or childhood friends years deep into a relationship. We weren't even the same age or from the same hood. We didn't have that type of foundation to fall back on, so we were forced to get real close, real fast because major creative and business decisions had to be made. It's pretty amazing that two artists so young were able to quickly form a bond to help each other navigate all the obstacles and opportunities over the years we were together.

Like most close relationships, a lot of it went smooth until some days it didn't. One of those days came on an early trip to our first record label Zakia in a meeting to talk about upcoming shows, among other things. While we were there, one of the executives came in to talk to Eric about some money he had given him. Now usually, when Eric was given an envelope, I got one the same day, same size, same weight. But this time, they were definitely talking about some paper exchanging hands, and I knew I hadn't seen any of it. I started steaming, my mind racing through what kind of side deals this guy has going on while I got no one watching. I called my brother Ronnie to come get me and while he sped across town, I confronted Eric in the hall. Maybe because he could see how angry I was getting, Eric just sort of stood there and wasn't really explaining anything. I got so mad that if Ronnie hadn't arrived as quickly as he did, it would have been the end of Eric B. & Rakim right there.

It turned out that Eric wasn't doing any side deal that day though. The money was actually for production expenses—turntables, mixers, and other things for our upcoming shows. But it still bothered me that I didn't know what was going on. Part of that was connected to the roles we had unofficially established for ourselves in the group. I was focusing on what I saw as my purpose and trying to outdo the last rhymes I had written, building bigger monuments. I think Eric saw a larger role for himself industry wide. He loved the business side of things as well as the music, so he gravitated to putting the deals together and handling the behind-the-scenes activities. But driving away from Zakia that day I realized that while he might sometimes take a bigger role in our group's corporate affairs, it didn't mean I wanted him managing my own business. I looked at Ronnie and said, "Man, I'm tired. I want to call Russell."

Russell Simmons was then the biggest manager in hip-hop. He represented the number-one group at the time, Run-DMC, which included his brother RUN, and along with Rick Rubin, founded one of the biggest hip-hop labels, Def Jam, the home of LL Cool J and the Beastie Boys. My brother knew Russell from having played in Kurtis Blow's band on tour. They used to share a hotel room a couple of nights a week to save some money while traveling. He called Russell from a pay phone. An hour later we were in his office. We talked about music.

"Do you have any choruses?" Russell asked.

"Choruses? You mean, like, with singers?"

At that point all I knew was beats and rhymes. I knew nothing about song structure. But this meeting wasn't really about music. I was in Russell's office silently deciding whether or not to stick with Eric. I could've signed a deal to let Russell manage me as a solo artist, and he would've gotten me out of my contract with Eric. I would've never had to talk to Eric again. I would be my own man. But deep in my gut I knew that was the wrong way to get that freedom. I had come this far because of Eric—if he hadn't introduced me to Marley Marl and walked us into Zakia and gotten our record on the radio, then I wouldn't have been in

Russell's office. I would have been at Stony Brook University. I couldn't lie to myself—it wasn't right abandoning him. No matter how much I questioned if what he was doing was for him or for us, I had to be able to respect myself. So I left the meeting and told Eric we should hire Russell's management company, Rush, to manage us. He agreed.

●●●

Eric rented a car and a week of studio time at Power Play Studios in Queens, and we started recording the rest of our debut album, *Paid in Full*. It cost forty-five dollars an hour. Every day that week we got to the studio around 5 p.m. and stayed until 9 a.m. Being in a real studio made me take these recordings more seriously. Seeing those big boards in that crisp, glittering studio made it really sink in that I was going to make records that lots of people would hear. I knew I had to be better than I'd ever been. I had to speak to people who didn't even know me. And somehow during that week at Power Play my talent took a quantum leap forward. I was great before we hit the studio, but that was nothing compared to what I did on that album. I was like an athlete walking into the biggest game of his career and playing in the zone.

Each time I went to the studio I didn't know what I was going to write. I started each session working on the beats. I did most of the music. Eric did all the scratches, but I did most of the beats. I pulled them from records I had rhymed over back when I was in the park. Eric did the instrumental songs—that was all him— but I did almost everything on the records I rhymed on.

On the way to the studio that first time, a bunch of questions ran through my head. Some of my thoughts were: *Who's going to be the engineer and will I get along with him? Am I going to be able to work around him? What's his vibe?* I knew I was going to have to trust somebody. I got there, and the legendary Patrick "Disco Pat" Adams was sitting in the chair. From the rip, I had the utmost respect for him. He was an older cat, one of my elders, and right away I knew he knew what he was doing. I had no idea who he was when I walked into the studio, but he was cool about it. He didn't pull rank. He didn't get insulting with some "You don't know who I am?" attitude. He just introduced himself and said he was the sound engineer. I introduced myself. We sat down and talked for a minute and then got to work.

As the days went on, we started talking during the sessions.

"You listen to music?" he asked me about two, three sessions in.

"Yeah."

"You ever heard 'In the Bush'?"

"Hell yeah. It's 'Push, push in the bush.' Everybody heard that track."

"Yeah, I made that."

"You made 'In the Bush'?"

"Yeah, I produced it. I made it."

"Word, brother. It's a provocative song," I said, trying not to lose it, but I was blown away with that.

Then he started telling me he made a bunch of other incredible music that was wildly popular, like "Hot Shot," "Caught Up," "Don't Turn Around," "Keep on Jumping," and "Atmosphere Strut." And he told me stories about making the tracks and what had been going on. He said that at the time nobody was making music like that. He talked about the ways the labels were kind of pushing back and didn't want to put them out. So he put them out on his own, and they were big hits.

I was wowed that he'd produced all these songs. After he shared this with me, I just sat there thinking, I got a legend in control. If I ain't one of the luckiest artists alive. He was cool as hell to get along with, and because of that, I was comfortable and able to try out whatever I wanted. It was dope that he was that cat. He made me feel real comfortable around him. And since he was a musician, it was even easier for me to bounce ideas off him. And to get his feedback and approval was real good for my confidence in my work. It was a dope experience.

Once I had the beat, I sat at the console and wrote rhymes with a pencil. I used a pencil because I did a lot of erasing. Usually it took me about an hour to get a verse done. I didn't write about my personal story. I wanted to write universal stories that everyone could relate to. I tried to write so the listener could find themselves in my rhymes. I wanted each member of the audience to feel like I was speaking directly to them. If I could make them think the song was for them, they'd love it.

I remember staring at a blank sheet of paper and wanting to take my writing to another level. Most of us write from left to right, but a voice in my head wondered if there was a different way to approach the page. For a radio song, the verses had to be sixteen bars, but I was used to writing verses that went a lot longer than that, so I started diagramming the paper with dots to represent time. When I knew how much time I had left, I saw how deep I could go into an idea or if I should start building up for the ending. It also led me to look at the page in a new way. Suddenly it seemed really boring to rhyme only on the fourth beat. I thought, *If I write the words in a different way, will that make the rhymes come out different?* I drew three lines down the page, creating a grid with four cells. Then I wrote horizontally and vertically, rhyming words that were in the second cell and the fourth cell or rhyming the second cell in one line with the second cell in the following line. I first wrote the rhyming words, then filled in the connecting words. That's how I came up with internal rhymes—when I found a new way to write, I found new possibilities.

I wrote "I Ain't No Joke" with lots of internal rhymes. It starts "I ain't no joke. I used to let the mic smoke. / Now I slam it when I'm done and make sure it's broke. / When I'm gone no one gets on 'cause I won't let / nobody press up and mess up the scene I set." In the first line I rhymed "joke" and "smoke." Then I made the third and fourth line lines mirror each other, giving you a pair of internal rhymes and then rhyming words at the ends of the lines. In the third line I rhymed "gone" with "gets on" in the same place where in the fourth line I rhyme "press up" and "mess up," and both lines come together with "I won't let" and "scene I set." A couple of lines later I rhymed in between the lines with "I'm just an addict addicted to music. / Maybe it's a habit, I gotta use it." So "addict" and "habit" rhyme with each other as well as "music" and "use it." I loved building rhymes out of words that don't really rhyme. I was always pushing myself to find new ways to connect words.

Then I began using those dots on the page to represent the places where I would take a breath. At first it was so I could get through the whole rhyme without running out of breath, but I quickly learned to put those rest dots in places where it would add syncopation so the pause would become part of the rhythm and the rhyme. Once I realized that the spaces in between the words could be just as important as the words or the notes, then I felt like I was totally in control of what I was doing with the pen and the mic. Those little silences can really affect people. Sometimes I was saying something that wasn't that deep, but my pauses and my tones infused it with more power.

I never wanted nobody to hear me gasp for air like a preacher deep into his sermon running out of breath. If you listen through most of my songs, you never hear that—let alone me taking a deep breath. You never hear me take a breath at all. In the beginning, I wondered if music listeners were knowledgeable of it. Then one day I heard some folks on the radio discussing hip-hop and they mentioned my name and were giving me praises. "Yo, my man got the breathless flow. You never hear him take it." It made me realize that some people were listening. So my advice to aspiring MCs and writers of all kinds is don't be scared to implement new approaches, because people may not catch on at first, but through time even the little things will stand out.

I found out where to take a breath through the whole song. And I put a dot with a yellow highlighter in each place, so as I was rhyming I would see the dot coming up. When the sound engineer recognized the difference and I told him what I did, he was impressed with the way I was able to flip it and make it work. "Yo, that's genius," he told me.

When I wrote that first album, I saw myself as a door-to-door salesman who needed a product that a lot of people could connect with. I tried to visualize my audience and think about who they were and what they wanted to hear. I was writing for people like me who love hip-hop, respect the culture, and enjoy thinking deeply about things.

I wanted to write deep things, which meant I had to put a lot of thought into each word. The only way for me to do that was to write in silence. I'd listen to the track many times really loud, then hit PAUSE and write when it was quiet so I could hear all of the thoughts going through my mind as I was creating. When I was writing, all these voices would pop up and start talking all at once, suggesting a hundred different directions the song could go in. I needed to be able to hear all of them clearly so I could find the right way to go.

I discovered that the beginning of a song was critical. I wanted to start by saying something memorable, with an opening line that would stick in your mind. But my tone was a big part of it too. I had to come in all smooth and calm, like I had everything under control. That would make people want to follow me. I took that easing-into-it approach with all the songs on *Paid in Full*. On the title track, I smoothed in with a soft tone in the first verse: "Thinkin' of a master plan . . ." It was like I was lightly dabbing the canvas to start the painting. I wanted to reel the audience in with my confidence, so in the first moments of the song I tried to give them a sense of "I'm cool."

The ending of a song depended on how I felt and what I needed to complete the theme. Sometimes I slowly declined into a calm tone in the last few bars of a song. Sometimes I built up steam toward the end and got more explosive. It depended on the concept of the song and the effect I was trying to achieve. It was all about what would help complete the theme or pattern I set up earlier.

The chorus should be just a few words, nothing too complicated, something nice and catchy. I need it to be less complex than the verses because the chorus is for the crowd to say. The verses are for me.

I find the best way to record is straight through. Not punching in a few lines here and then a few more lines there. I just get in the booth and kick the whole verse all at once so I can create a whole sonic environment with my words and tones and pacing and pausing and everything. I recorded all the verses on *Paid in Full* in either two or three passes. Never more than that. On all of those songs you hear me in a single recording. I rhymed the whole verse—straight through—like a real MC should.

The last song we made that week was "Paid in Full." It was a song for the masses, meant to encourage and inspire people. I painted a picture of someone hitting rock bottom and having nothing, and I was telling him, *Hey, I see you. Keep fighting, man.* My pops used to say, "If you go down the street looking for a job and you don't get a job, you should go home, wake up the next morning, shower, and then go in the opposite direction." "Paid in Full" was a message to keep going. I wanted to uplift people. The song was my cure for the world.

CONSCIOUSNESS

Musical Massacre

How could I keep my composure
when all sorts of thoughts fought for exposure?
Release, then veins in the brains increase.
When I let off, make a wish, and blow the smoke off my piece.
Unloadin', unfoldin', and the rhymes are exploding.
And the mic that I'm holding is golden.
Cordless cause the wire caught fire like a fuse.
Gunpowder and the slightest bruise is a friction.
The outcome is near so listen.
Here's the brief description.
A boom then flame then smoke, ashes and dust to dust.
Contact is compact when I bust.
MCs are now in a massacre.
A disaster a . . . master at bashin' a beat to death,
to a pulp, till it can't pump.
Speakers ain't saying nothing.
Now a volt can thump.
As I'm looking I stand like great buildings in Brooklyn.
Then the stage is tooken, then

havoc struck that could product a holocaust

Keep in touch with the mic when you're holding y'all.

Huffing and puffing and slobbing and drooling,

nothing's pumping, who do you think you're fooling?

Tommy tucker, the neighborhood sucker,

what you ought to do . . . is pick up a tempo.

From what I invent, so hard not to bite, but you can't
    prevent so

you start to kidnap.

I watch the kid rap.

When he get off he know he shouldn'ta did that.

Minor, old-timer, weak-rhymer, stay-in-liner.

You won't be inclined to go so yo

maybe later, you're going to be,

but for now, you're almost one of me.

Now the immature imitations taken from originations,

made by tracing and a little erasing.

So perform, if you still ain't warm maybe after.

A roast by the host with the most, it's a musical massacre.

Never tired, don't even try it, keep quiet.

Like a storm, you could rain . . . but a riot

remains to gain power just like the towering inferno.

The beat's going to burn so

distance is kept, you better watch your step.

Volunteers won't come here to get

you out of the flames.

Preheat the temperature change

Anywhere within the range of Celsius.

Fahrenheit on the mic, might melt see it's

burnt soon as it's felt see it's torchin', scorchin'.

Mic's piping hot, steaming who's scheming now you're not.

James Brown must have been dusted.

Disgusted, now he can't be trusted.

Embalmed with fluid,

static can cause explosion, in fact impact's closing in.

Time was up, so I release a time bomb.

Beat gives me a heatstroke but I rhyme calm.

Pull out the tool, sometimes I want to break fool.

But I was cool, like one in the chamber.

Let's play a game of rhyming roulette

and put me up to your brain and name a rhyme about
   your clout.

One mistake . . . you're out.

It's a demonstration it can't be the same show.

Maybe you too fly somewhere over the rainbow.

Courage, heart, and brains, you need rhyme.

Turn on your mic, snap your fingers three times.

Be gone, or the story won't end the same

and you'll feel the flame.

The potion was weak, make another antidote.

What's the science? Why can't you quote?

Elements with musical intelligence.

Rhymes are irrelevant, no development.

And that settles it.

Go manufacture a match, send me after a blast.

Of a massive, it has to make musical massacre.

Notes on "Musical Massacre"

"Musical Massacre" was the hardest song to make on our second album. We thought we were finished, and we handed the album in. But the record company said we needed one more song. We were supposed to go to the Grammys, which were being held at Radio City Music Hall in New York City. When they said we needed a new song, my mind flipped back into song mode, and when it comes to having to go somewhere or having to do a record, I don't like to do both. It's always been like that. I don't like to spread myself too thin. I like to focus on what I'm doing. If I'm writing, then I want to focus on that. If it takes me a full day to do what I have to do, then that's cool. At this time I was writing songs right in the studio. In fact, the majority of that album I wrote right at the studio. A couple of times I might write two verses, then go home, and come back the next day and write a third verse. But not knowing how long it was going to take me to write a song was partially why the pressure to get it done was so stressful. I was lucky things were flowing the way they were. But there was no way I would assume that I could go to the Grammys—or for that matter do a show, do a photo shoot, or go out to eat with the label—and then by 10:00 p.m. go to the studio and a write a hit and be out by four in the morning. That wasn't my MO at all. I'd rather go in by 11:00 a.m. and work all day, and if it just so happened, work till seven in the morning. But I'd go home with a finished song. And that was my way of rocking. I was a young perfectionist. I still am.

Eric B. went to the Grammys. I stayed back to finish the

song. Because we thought we were done, I had already shut down mentally. So now I'm thinking, *Another one? Damn, I don't even know if I have another song in me.* I didn't really have any more records in mind to sample. We had used all of them joints I had rapped over back in the day—the ones I was in love with. I was thinking, *What am I gonna do now?* But I found something, and I did "Musical Massacre" that night.

I picked the record "It's Just Begun" by the Jimmy Castor Bunch because it was a big B-boy record. Break-dancers loved it. But as I was sampling it and everything was coming together, I realized that it was not an easy record to rhyme to. I think it was the tempo; it was way fast. But knowing we had a deadline looming, I kept working at it. The process was like real organic. Even though I didn't know how to approach the rhyming, I got up in the studio, pulled that record out, sampled it up. I came up with the title, and as I fleshed out the idea for the song further, I had a little idea. Eric B. would probably get mad, but I decided to scratch some records onto the track. That was my DJ debut. Eric B. wasn't there, so I did the scratching on the record! Then I sat there, wrote my rhyme, and went in the booth.

The style was real different from anything I had ever done. So everything about the whole session was a little off. It came out dope. But it's still one of them records where every now and then when I'm performing, I hear someone in the audience yell out, "Musical Massacre!" And I'm like, "What do you guys know about that?!"

EMBRACE CONSCIOUS ENERGY

Performance days are an important part of being a hip-hop artist. Their value to the art shouldn't be diminished. For a hip-hop artist, the writing is when you're in the trenches: that's the hard part. But performance is the best part. The performance is also an opportunity for your fans to gain a better understanding of your art than what they are able to experience from just hearing it or seeing a music video. And for the artist, it's always good to get onstage and express that work you put in. That's when you get a chance to experiment with different approaches, have fun with it, converse with the crowd, share different insights on your artistic process, and get feedback. Likewise, by paying attention to the crowd, you also learn which of your songs has the most impact.

During the day of a show, I come down early and play some music first. I love going through my crates and playing all sorts of different records. Get in the mood, and get my energy flowing. It makes it easy to put my head where it needs to be and almost visualize myself in the building, theater, nightclub, or wherever, onstage and in front of the crowd. From there you can start implementing your vision for what you want to do that evening. You got your third eye on, and you're basically trying to picture how it's going to be. You start getting the feel of it. Make sure your intro record is big. You want a nice intro that is theatrical and lets the crowd know right out the gate "That dude is here." Next, I set up my records according to crowd impact. I try to make sure the show has good peaks and valleys. You have to know when to slow it down and, most important, how to pick it back up. Because I have up-tempo records and slow records that the crowd likes to hear me perform as well, I try to mix up my show where it's a good combination of slow BPM songs and fast-paced joints. I try to put it together and feel my show out in my head. I sit there. I vibe on it. Make sure that it feels right. I'll test it, play the records in the order I want them to line up. It's one of them things where you have to see it all beforehand and bring it into alignment with what you feel is going to be a good show.

I've been performing for decades, and no matter how many times I do it, the ambition to go out and rip the room down never diminishes. You want to make sure you give a good show. You want everybody leaving saying it was an amazing night. I love to block everything out and just focus on that sense of responsibility to do my personal best. Nothing matters except getting on that stage and getting off with a successful show. After that, I can be normal again. I can remember what's going on around me, what's going on in my life. But on that stage nothing matters. You're waiting for them records to come on. You're waiting to hear that crowd. You're waiting to hear if they're going to respond to what you're doing. You're waiting to see if tonight is the night when you can do anything onstage and the crowd will just go crazy.

BEYOND BUTTERFLIES

I like to be relaxed before a show. I don't like to be stressed out. I don't like to take bad energy onstage. You want to be on point. Well rested. Make sure your wardrobe is right. You want to be focused, and try to have your energy up so you can project that into the crowd.

If you're serious about your art, you will inevitably experience what people refer to as butterflies in your stomach. Don't run away from that. In fact, the less you experience that sensation is not especially the better. I like to think of it not as butterflies but as conscious energy. I remember when I was in elementary school playing on the Police Athletic League and Pop Warner football teams. One day my father was taking me to a game. I was sitting there kind of quiet, I guess. Wasn't talking. Pops asked me if I had butterflies, and I didn't really know what that meant.

"You got butterflies?" he asked.

"Huh?"

"You nervous?" he probed further.

"Yeah, a little bit." Before the games I used to get butterflies, but I hadn't known what they were.

"That's not nervousness, that's consciousness," he said.

"You understand what you're about to do is serious to you. You're about to play a game, and you want to win the game. You're not scared, are you?"

"No, I'm not scared, Pop."

"Well, then that's not nervousness, that's consciousness."

That taught me how to get rid of my butterflies right there—at the young age of seven. Once I found out what it meant, and once my father gave me that confidence, I pretty much put what other people think of as butterflies behind me.

CROWD ENERGY

Once you step onstage, hear the crowd, see the crowd, and feel that crowd energy, you forget everything. Sharing that energy with the audience is one of the craziest things about performing. When I come offstage, I can't sleep for at least five, six hours, that energy is so incredible. I remember one time I hurt my knee, and I was limping around all day. I went and got a knee brace. Still limping around. As the day went on and I was realizing that I was really going to have to limp onstage that night, I decided I was going to have to let the crowd know that I'd hurt my knee so they would understand why I was limping around. Limped the rest of the day. Limped to the building. Limped to the dressing room. Got onstage and didn't limp one time. I couldn't even feel my knee. I forgot that my knee was hurting. It's unexplainable, but I attribute that to crowd energy. There's something about it that supersedes everything.

That energy makes me forget everything I might've gone

through or what I'm even currently going through. I try my best to be in good spirits before I get onstage, but no matter what, it's a good thing that the energy from the crowd is so crazy. If I'm in a bad mood, I forget that immediately. It's the crowd and me, and it's positive. Get offstage and get back to the dressing room. Start limping again. And then everything else starts coming back too. But for that hour and a half, you're numb.

When the opportunity to perform arises, your emotions are as high as hell. You're doing what you love best. You're expressing something you put so much blood, sweat, and tears into. And to get complimented for that by your fans is an emotional rush.

Sometimes you get onstage and the crowd goes crazy, and you feel like you can do nothing wrong. You can almost do nothing and kill it. Other times, the crowd is a little more laid-back and you have to work harder. You have to move around. You have to wake them up. You have to talk to them. You have to yell at them. You have to be forceful. You have to perform your songs a little harder and kind of reverse the favor: rather than the crowd initiating this energy and you performing for them, sometimes you have to get out there and give that crowd the spark, and they'll respond to you.

IT AIN'T WHERE YOU'RE FROM, IT'S WHERE YOU'RE AT

There are always different moods in different places. Some places like different songs. Sometimes you can go in a building and use certain rhymes or call outs to get a crowd response. Some cities know these sayings; some cities don't. Sometimes you have to tell the crowd what to say. Sometimes you just blurt out the beginning lyrics of one of your rap songs and they finish it for you. It's like one of those things that come from out of nowhere. Unexpected. In some of the big cities, certain trends are more prevalent. New York, Chicago, Detroit, Miami, Houston, California, Atlanta—at these places, you can go in there and kind of show off because it's hip-hop oriented. Big tours go through the cities a lot, so they often get the code—more so than smaller cities and suburbs beyond the mainstream.

Early on in my career, I always wrote rhymes from a New York point of view because that's all I knew. When I started going on tour, seeing different places, and seeing how different places do what they do—everything from how they dress, how they talk, how they live, how their city looks, how they party—it gave me a broader view. That realization inspired me to create the expression "It ain't where you're from, it's where you're at," which I first rhymed in my song "In the Ghetto." If I'm in New York, I can get onstage and say several things and New York knows exactly what it is. In New York I can put my hand in my pocket and look at the crowd and they go crazy. But you go to another city and they don't get it. You have to speak their language. "It ain't where you're from." I'm from New York, but I may be deep down in Louisiana or way over in Omaha. In Nashville you have to come out and do something. Maybe I have to dance a little bit. I need to speak a slightly different language so they understand me. I had to learn to adapt to different environments and situations to be a little more universal. Make sure that onstage you speak the language of "where you're at" at all times.

The size of the venue can also shift the performing experience. For example, you can do a show for 10,000, 15,000, 20,000 people and it's crazy. In a big arena, you could basically stand up there, close your eyes, and do the whole show. And nobody will really care that you got your eyes closed, 'cause you up there rocking. But then sometimes you go to the smaller clubs—300, 400, 500 people—and have a whole different feeling. Unlike in a big arena, the crowd in the small, intimate spots is fifteen feet from the stage. You're right there, more up close and personal, so you have to be touchable. They can reach out and grab your pants leg. Eye contact is important. Interacting with the crowd is important: the conversing with the crowd, the back and forth, the organic conversations. But what doesn't change is that energy, as well as your passion about performing.

PERFORMING HELPS BUILD THE ART

Being serious about my craft, my art, my brand, extends to how I represent it when I'm onstage. It has to be understood that the performance itself is also part of the art. It's imperative that the show goes well. If it doesn't, afterward you feel like you cheated the crowd. You feel like you failed. At that point you can blame whatever happened only on yourself. Because at the end of the day, when the show ends and they all head home, all they remember is who was onstage.

If the record skips, or the record stops, you got two choices: take it back to the top or chalk it up and go to the next record. If you choose to start that record from the beginning, the smart way to do it is to bring the crowd along. Set it up in a way that makes the show feel organic: "Yo, we going take it from the top. I want y'all to act like . . ." Get them involved and they will respond.

REMEMBER YOUR PURPOSE

As much as it's important to represent your art and brand onstage, the same is true offstage while touring. Again, this is hip-hop! If it's your first time out on the road, be prepared for the unique variety of challenges that come with being a rap artist. A lot of things out there can detour you from what you're supposed to be doing: women, drugs, late hours, lost highways, and a whole lot of other distractions. You want to make sure that you focus and avoid serious trouble. You don't want to get sidetracked and do something stupid with your friends, a random girl you met, get into a fight, get arrested. And it gets worse than that. The first time I went on tour I was just eighteen years old. You can bet I made some mistakes. I was both lucky and trying to be as cautious as I could. My upbringing helped. Let's just say Mom and Pop didn't raise no fool. To this day, I still have fun, but not too much fun.

Remember why you're making music, and recognize that the people who support you are the most important people to you. I'm not saying that you have to go over to everybody's house and take a hundred selfies with them. But realizing what you're doing it for goes back to staying focused and finding your purpose. Just as you respect your craft and your purpose, never forget that your fans are the ones who make you a star: they are the ones supporting your career, buying your music, attending your concerts. Acknowledge this by making sure you show them respect. Appreciate them when they come up to you and give you all that love. Sometimes it might be a little overwhelming. You might have a lot on your plate. Their enthusiasm may make it seem as if they don't care what you're going through in that given moment. I'm not saying it's all right for them not to care. But you're the one who sat in the crib trying to amaze everybody. Now that you've done it, that's supposed to be their reaction. Handle it with respect and a little understanding. I promise you, it will go a long away.

FROM HIGH SCHOOL
TO RAP STAR

F or months before our first album, *Paid in Full*, had hit the streets—we were doing three or four club gigs every weekend, often two or three clubs a night in New York or Connecticut or Virginia or North Carolina. We got $7,500 a show, so we often made over $20,000 in a weekend. It was easy money—we didn't practice our show or plan out what we'd do, we just got up there and whatever happened was okay.

In January of 1987 Eric came to the crib and said, "Ra, you're gonna have to leave school."

I looked at him like he was crazy.

"Ra, it's serious," Eric said. "The record is blowing up faster than anyone expected. We gotta go on tour to capitalize on the heat we got going right now. We can't wait until the summer. We gotta go now."

"How am I gonna explain this to my mom?"

"Man, we're gonna make serious money."

He said we were looking at getting $12,500 a show on the '87 Def Jam Tour with a who's who of the rap universe: Public Enemy, Whodini, Doug E. Fresh, Stetsasonic, and, of course, the headliner, LL Cool J, the biggest solo star in the game at that time.

This was my chance to be a real professional rapper, but the decision to leave school was a major one and this time it was not going to be mine alone. I had to get the okay from my parents. They went off to their room to talk about it.

Because my father had been a music manager, he knew what it meant for an artist to strike while the iron was hot. He used to say, "When the phone is ringing a lot, answer it. You never know when they'll stop calling." He agreed with Eric that I had to go now. Moms disagreed. She wanted me to finish high school. She understood the opportunity the tour offered, she knew I was going to make good money, but music careers could be short. Who would I be in ten years without a high school degree? They argued for a while. They called Aunt Ruth to get her opinion. "Let him go for it," she said. Mom reluctantly said okay.

My father gave me tons of advice about what to expect on tour and how to make good decisions. He told me entertainers don't really have a personal life—I would have to give myself to the fans all the time.

Just because mom agreed didn't mean she wasn't very upset. She hated the idea of me not graduating from high school on time. She felt like I was risking my future. "You're making a decision you may regret in the future. Promise me you'll get your GED."

I promised her.

Felicia said she had a bad feeling about me going on the road. She didn't really want to see her boyfriend go away on tour and have chicks scream at him every night. She was proud of me, but she was afraid this would end our relationship. She wanted me to go because it was good for my music, but she didn't expect me to go on tour and be mature. She reminded me that at home I'd been smoking and carrying guns and cutting school—what was she supposed to expect from me when I was on tour? I promised her I was not going to get into trouble.

I tried to live up to both of my promises. I really did. But I never went back to school. Overnight my life shifted from cheap basement studios and the streets of Wyandanch to professional studios and big stages around the country. In a flash I went from high school senior to real rap star. One day I was asking Moms if I could I go to Delancey Street and the next I was getting on a plane to Miami. I had an entire crew of people taking my directions, a pocket full of cash, and people cheering for me and my rhymes wherever I went. I felt like a king.

Big tours are filled with big temptations. There are all sorts of things floating around, all sorts of trapdoors that lead to trouble. You have men who are quick to pull out a weapon to prove their manhood and their loyalty, and people who will cater to your ego, while watching your wallet. There are drugs that'll cure your anxieties about failing or your need for adrenaline or whatever trip you want to take. I remembered how much trust my parents had shown in letting me leave school to pursue this, and I knew I had promised Felicia that I would not get into trouble. There were temptations I had to battle and I wasn't always perfect, but I felt lucky to sidestep the pitfalls that can twist most people up.

My biggest challenge was preparing myself to perform on a much bigger stage alongside artists who already had the experience. That whole tour I was trying to make my stage show better. I was a laid-back dude who liked to rhyme in the park for a few hundred people, and now I was in arenas trying to control the attention of twenty or thirty thousand. I had a lot to learn. When we weren't onstage, I stood in the wings watching other acts and taking little cues and hints, but I was mostly watching the crowd and how they reacted to different moments of the show.

Every night the energy blew me away. We quickly realized that everything was choreographed and rehearsed, but you had to make it look new every time.

I loved performing, but I was so calm and cool onstage that my audience couldn't be certain that I really wanted to be up there. After years of fighting to be laid back, I had to learn how to amp myself up a bit. It was cool to be low-energy on records, but onstage I was coming across too casual. I had to bring more energy to the performance. It took me time to learn how to project energy and power without raising my voice. I ended up using a sharp, strong tone that made my voice carry in large spaces but didn't take away from what I was saying. I also had to know how to take advantage of the big-energy moments of my songs, and I had to pay more attention to how I expressed excitement to the audience. I didn't dance, but it's not about dancing. Every onstage movement communicates something. If you don't dance, that sends a message. But I had to have some sort of physical conversation with the crowd. I had to move around in hip-hop ways and act out scenes and make gestures that helped punctuate the records. I had to have alpha body language at all times. When I'm onstage rhyming, I'm the leader, the commander of the ship, and I've gotta let everyone know that it's my house and I'm in charge. I've gotta make eye contact and give the crowd things to say—the name of their city or a word or something. I want to make them feel like they're part of the show and we're creating this moment together.

I had to give the audience more than just words. I had to give them an experience. I got into walking onstage and just standing there with my arms crossed, wearing a look of supreme confidence on my face. Over time we managed to come up with a show that we didn't practice but it was uniform night after night. I knew what I was supposed to do when each song came on.

You've also got to be ready for the unexpected. If a record skips, there are three things I can do. I can wait, listen, and catch up with the beat. Or I can say, "Yo. Hold up. Bring that back, man. Start from the beginning." Or I can panic and yell at the DJ and the sound man and stop the show and make the whole team look unprofessional. I always chose to roll with the punches and keep the show going no matter what. Fix it without letting the audience know. Some young artists make things worse by telling the crowd that someone else caused the problem. I saw rappers onstage say that the soundman sucked or someone else messed something up, but if they hadn't said that, nine out of ten times the crowd wouldn't have known there was a problem! If something goes wrong, try to pretend like nothing happened.

Every night was a different challenge. There was always a chance that things could go haywire. I could fall on my face. I could forget a rhyme. The sound could cut out. Anything could happen, so I had to be on top of everything. Sometimes on the way to the show I'd look at the set list. My peoples would say, "What are you doing? It's the same show from last night and the night before that and the night before that!" But I wanted to be sure. I never assumed it would all work out. I never got cocky about the stage. I never went into a show feeling like it was going to be all good. I had to stay ready for anything. I was projecting ego to the crowd, but I was humble about the whole situation because there were so many ways I could mess up. And everyone was waiting to see the new guy stumble in some way. But I never did. Except for the time when before the show in Miami I got drunk with the legendary Uncle Luke from 2 Live Crew and went onstage and couldn't remember my lyrics. I can barely remember that night at all.

I also learned quickly that it's not just on stage where things might go wrong. If you don't handle yourself well after the show things can go off the rails. A lot of nights after shows, me and Eric and the crew would go out in the streets around a venue and find the bootleggers who were selling lots of merchandise— mostly T-shirts with our faces on them. We would see them before the show, setting up, and take note but not say anything to them. They would sit out there for hours. At the end of the show, we'd jump them and take the remaining T-shirts and all of their money. And sometimes they didn't want to comply. We used to beat it out of them. The way I saw it, all those shirts were ours and all that money was ours. They were selling unlicensed product with our faces on them—that's stealing from us! One particular time in Philadelphia we rolled into the parking lot of the old Spectrum arena and found the T-shirt sellers and just started whipping ass. I clocked a few dudes right in the face. When the cops came, people pointed at me, and the next thing I knew I was in a holding cell. I knew my people were making calls and doing everything they could to get me out, but I was sitting in there, watching the clock, thinking, *The show is gonna start in two hours . . . Damn . . . The show is starting in thirty minutes . . . And here I go just sitting!*

But then someone called my man Joe Frazier, the Philly-based boxing legend. I was friends with Joe's nephew, and we all used to go to the fights together and stop by his uncle's gym to hang out. So Joe really knew me. I was a friend of the family so Joe stuck his neck out and called the precinct.

An officer came to my cell and said, "We're gonna let you out and take you to your concert."

One minute I was locked up and the next I was in the back of a police car racing to my show with the lights blaring as we sliced through traffic. At the back entrance, I jumped out of the car, strutted into the building, and walked straight to the stage. The roar was as loud as I've ever heard.

THE HIP-HIP
THRONE

As our Def Jam Tour crossed the country, the Together Forever Tour, starring Run-DMC and the Beastie Boys, was also traveling nationally. They were hip-hop royalty. Everybody loved Run-DMC. They had swagger, they had flavor, they were cool, and they made so many hits. Run-DMC took hip-hop to a new level—first rappers to go platinum, first rappers to do *The Tonight Show* with Johnny Carson, first rappers to do *Saturday Night Live*. They constantly reset the benchmark for success in the rap game, and I had to respect that lyrically I knew I was more complex.

Once we ended up at the same hotel, and after the show I got drinks with Jam Master Jay, the DJ and the heart of the group. The clothing style they adopted with the fedoras, the gold rope chains, the dark denim suits, and the shell toes, that was Jay's normal look. We drank Hennessy, and he talked about how to avoid the rap-star big-head syndrome. He told me to remember they were not cheering for me, they were cheering for the music. The day they don't like the music is the day they stop cheering. He told me to be grounded and grateful and never forget that my success is because I'm a talented person, not because I'm a better person than anyone else.

While we were on tour our debut album *Paid in Full* came out and exploded. A new single, "I Ain't No Joke," backed with "I Know You Got Soul," blew up on the radio and in the clubs and in the cars. We were selling thousands of vinyl records and cassettes and CDs a week. Island Records, a pretty big label, saw that our record was blowing up and getting too big for a little company like Zakia Records to handle, so Island picked up our option. Island was the home of reggae giants—Bob Marley, Jimmy Cliff, Toots and the Maytals—but they had no major hip-hop acts. They put us on 4th and B'way, their subsidiary label that focused on hip-hop. Now we had some real marketing dollars pushing us and a distributor who could put hundreds of thousands of albums into stores. Over the next six months we sold more than 500,000 albums, a truckload for a hip-hop album then. We weren't the biggest stars in the game, but people were saying I was the best MC out, and I was still pushing myself to get better. One of the main reasons I never felt competition from other rappers was because I was only competing with myself, which also kept me pretty humble. I had an alter ego that would dismiss others as inferior wordsmiths. If I saw a rapper out in a club, I wouldn't speak to him. I might nod, but I definitely wasn't hanging out and having a conversation. In those days there was so much competitive energy it was impossible to be chummy. I knew that when they wrote they were thinking about my rhymes and trying to outdo me lyrically and take my spot, so I wasn't interested in befriending them. My alter ego wanted people to fear me, but I just kept trying to improve and really didn't pay much attention to others.

■ ■ ■

We got an offer from Island Records to do our second album for $450,000.

"Hell no," Eric said. He was the leader of the business side of the group. We'd sold over a million records. He said, "Our record is more profitable than *Joshua Tree*." That was U2's smash.

Island said, yes, it was, but "it's rap music."

"Isn't rap money the same color as U2 money?"

Island stood firm at $450,000.

Two nights later, we were out at a club and we ran into Mike Haley from MCA Records, one of the biggest labels in the industry. He asked what we were doing for our second album.

"Island's trying to sign us for $450,000," Eric said.

"Don't sign nothing," Mike replied.

A day or so later, Eric told Russell that MCA was interested in us.

"You got half a million dollars on the table from Island. You wanna pass that up?"

"Let's just see what they have to say," Eric responded.

"MCA ain't got no rap artists," Russell told him. "$450,000 is the most a rapper has ever gotten for an album. Run-DMC doesn't get $450,000 for their albums!"

"No disrespect, but we weren't talking about Run-DMC. We were talking about Eric B. & Rakim and how we need you to focus on the best situation for us."

The next day we flew to LA and met with the execs at MCA. When we got back to the hotel, they called Lyor Cohen, Russell's business partner. They offered us an $800,000 signing bonus as part of a five-album deal with a recording budget of $1 million for our next album and an escalating budget for the following albums. We were shocked, but Lyor wasn't—he was tall, tough, intense, and a great negotiator. A little while later he told us Warner Bros. had called. We didn't know anyone over there, but suddenly there was a bidding war over us.

Warner offered a $900,000 signing bonus. Then MCA offered a signing bonus of $1 million. The first million-dollar record deal in hip-hop. I also got a $2 million publishing deal for my songs. Just two years earlier I had no thought of ever making money as an MC, and now I was out buying a Benz, a Jeep Cherokee, jewelry, clothes, and sneakers.

I was the best MC in the game. I knew it, and I knew most MCs would admit it if they were telling the truth, so I wrote my second album as if I was sitting on the hip-hop throne. At that point I thought my biggest rivals on the mic were Big Daddy Kane and Kool G Rap. They were the lyricists I respected most. Kane was a Brooklyn MC who had a great, heavy voice and a way of rhyming fast and yet remaining precise at speed. I preferred slower tracks and the freedom they gave me to be creative—I always felt like a slower track had more space in which I could play. But I tipped my hat to Kane on that fast rapping. G Rap was a Queens MC who was great at mixing in multisyllabic words and gangster stories and ripping ill flows. He was definitely my kinda MC. The fans and the media definitely measured me against those guys and most of the time I won. But the only real measuring stick for my success and sense of accomplishment was myself. That competition never ended.

But my alter ego definitely wanted to finish off that G.O.A.T. debate, so I wrote "Follow the Leader" to capture this sense of where my peers were relative to me in the rap game. The beat from the Mandrill's song "Fat City Strut" inspired me. When I heard that beat, it made me want to say something deeper than I normally did. But I had to make sure people could follow me. The first thing that came to mind was the phrase "Follow the leader." I thought of those old TV commercials where a ball on the screen would bounce above the words so people could sing along. It was a corny idea, but that's how the song came about. I wanted people to follow the rhyme just as all the MCs were following me, so the first line of the song was "Follow me into a solo." After I put that down, I couldn't stop the pen from moving. I wrote all three verses in one sitting.

I started with "Follow me into a solo / Get in the flow / and you can picture like a photo," and I gave each phrase a different tone, drawing listeners in with the varying textures. Then I came back with a line of *m*'s: "music mixed mellow maintains the make / melodies for MCs, motivate the break." Then right after all those short *m* sounds I hit you with a long "I'm everlaaasting," which, after all those short *m*'s, explodes in the ear.

In the third verse I had to show someone who was boss. I said, "Stop bugging a brother said dig him, I never dug him. / He couldn't follow the leader long enough so I drug him." It was a shot at EPMD. In one song they mentioned "Dig 'Em Smack" so when I said, "dig him," everyone in hip-hop knew I was talking about them.

But before I got to writing my rhymes, we had to get the music right first.

"The sample's too noisy," I said to Pat Adams, who was also sound engineer for our second album.

"Let's just play it over the keys," Pat suggested.

All right. Good idea. Let's play it. My brother Stevie played the bass line, and I laid the beat down. For some reason the sampler wasn't working, so Stevie played that whole track and had to play it straight through without losing the timing once. After about two or three takes, we played the whole joint for like five minutes straight. We finally got the sampler to work, and we were able to lay the horns and the strings down. What was crazy is that I had the title and the track, but I didn't know how I was going to do it. But once I got in there, we threw Bob James "Nautilus" on it, and the sample just took me straight to imagining planets, like Saturn, and the solar system: *da da-da, da da-da, da-doom.* And then the horns: *bamp, bamp-bamp.*

When we were making it, we had put the 808 on the track. And I started telling Pat how I wanted it to sound:

"Yo, Pat, make it sound like this!" I said excitedly.

Pat hit some buttons and the sound and the samples just went crazy.

"Oh, Pat, see if you can maybe . . ."

Pat hit some more buttons. Boom-boom.

"Yo, Pat, make that like, instead of hitting frontwards, make it hit backwards, like vroom-vroom instead of boom-boom."

Pat did something and flipped it backwards and suddenly the air is sucking into the subwoofer instead of pushing out. It was so loud in the studio, and it was hitting so hard but it had zero distortion. And once Pat put on a bass, he started two-timing.

Everything was going vroom-vroom. It sounded like a dungeon door closing. About two minutes into the song, the whole studio went black. We shut the whole studio down with "Follow the Leader." Incredible. The entire studio. Every floor, every room, every hallway. We blew a circuit. Too much power. Pat had it sounding like nothing I'd ever heard before. It was incredible.

After they got the studio back up and running, we had to pull back a little bit because of what he had done. While we waited, I remember sitting in there and putting the track together and adding all the elements to it, and the first thing that came to my mind were the words "Follow me into a solo, get in the flow, / and you can picture like a photo." I probably wrote the whole track in two hours.

That was one of them joints where I felt like, *Don't ask me nothing. Don't stop the track. Don't talk too loud. If you want to get on the phone, that's the door to the hallway. If you want to talk, sit in the car. If you do come in here, shut the hell up and just listen.*

"Astray into the Milky Way, world's out of sight." Da da-da, da da-da, da-dnnnn. The way the music sounded right there, so otherworldly, is what made me write that. The song itself being so dope that it took me there. And now I was inviting my audience to try to envision what I was seeing, while I was saying it, to show them Earth spinning from a distance. In that video, we went the other way with it and did some gangsta theme, but the track was a journey into the cosmos.

That was the beginning of the second album. Making "Follow the Leader" definitely got me ready to see what else I could do.

While I was working on the *Follow the Leader* album, I fell into the habit of putting a lot of research into my rhymes. The pressure of knowing the world would listen to me made me feel like

I needed to read and think and know everything I could possibly know about a subject before I wrote a song about it. I may have used a quarter of the research I dug up, but I had to know everything before I could choose which quarter to use.

Once I thought about doing a song about the apocalypse, so I got out the Bible and read it for eight hours, then I read the Qur'an and I studied the Torah. I spent three days, eight hours a day, reviewing those religious texts, and five other books about spirituality and religion, just to put together sixteen bars. All that for a song that never even came out.

But I couldn't spend days and days on every rhyme. I had to get lots of songs done in a certain time frame, and sometimes I sat down with a pen and found myself paralyzed and couldn't shut down my inner doubt about what to write or whether I could live up to my standards. Some days I sat there for hours with a blank page as I doubted and second-guessed and struggled to write. You might call it writer's block, but I try not to use that term. I trained myself to believe that writer's block doesn't exist. But if I couldn't get going and my pen wouldn't move, it could mean that I needed to go out and live more and see more of the world. Sometimes I just needed to step away from the studio and load in some new sights by taking a drive through the city and look around at New York—the big buildings, the speed of the streets, the flair of my people as they strut down the block. Even a short whip around in my Benz could make me feel like I had new eyes and was ready to write.

But some days even that didn't work. That's when I tried writing backwards. I wrote the sixteenth bar, which contained the final lines of the verse, and then the fifteenth bar, and so on up to the first bar. Once I knew the destination, it was easier to build the ramp to it. But whenever I did that I felt like I was taking a shortcut around the creative process. Like I was using a cheat code. I felt almost embarrassed doing it. Then I watched a documentary where *The Godfather* director Francis Ford Coppola said if you want to write a good movie, start at the end and work your way up to the beginning. Then I knew I wasn't cheating. It was just a different way of approaching the page.

I wanted the overall vibe of the *Follow the Leader* album to be hardcore hip-hop that was rough and dark. Eric wanted to do more radio-friendly songs that were bright and chorus heavy. He seemed to have a vision that was setting us up for more commercial success. There was tension when we disagreed on direction.

We went shopping together before a video once, and he kept trying to buy suits. I liked getting my grown man on, but I thought we belonged in sweatsuits and sneakers, like our people. But for a while we worked things out. After going to a party thrown by our friends Rap and Preme, we got introduced to Fila suits and the custom street wear of the Harlem designer Dapper Dan. They were both fly and street enough to appeal to us both, so we hit every sports store in the boroughs to buy out the track suits and commissioned Dan to dress us for the cover of *Follow the Leader*. Those designs and the jewelry that came with our success became a signature look that was and still is frequently imitated.

I worked on *Follow the Leader* for a few months. "Lyrics of Fury," was one of the songs on the album that I've always thought of as my horror movie. My brother used to play George Clinton in the crib all the time. I was a little dude, and I remember this one song he used to play and the face I used to make when he used to play it. Like *What is this?* It sounded crazy. I never imagined I would rhyme off something like that. We did the beat with the James Brown drum, and I remember looking through the crates. I would sometimes sample a beat, but then I would go through the crate, play samples over the top of the beat, and see which one I wanted to sample. So I pulled George Clinton out 'cause I knew I wanted something crazy-sounding. I said, "Yo, put this one on and let's try it." As soon as we put it on I realized I had forgotten exactly how the record really sounded. That bass was crazy. The problem was, by the time the song got to that part, the tempo of the song had changed. We sampled it. Chopped it. I start listening to it, and after two minutes, three minutes, I said, "Lyrics of Fury." I was just seeing visions of horror flicks, 'cause it sounded like the music you hear when the boogie man is about to get you.

I love doing songs like "Lyrics of Fury"—my energy songs. Songs where I can get a little stress off my chest, air out on rappers, and kinda let 'em know: Don't think for a minute you can *touch* me.

What I am describing in this song is that the God MC was in the park with a boom box blasting, sitting there ready to murder you:

> I'm rated R, this is a warnin', you better void.
> Poets are paranoid, DJs destroyed.
> I came back to attack brothers that's bitin'.
> Strike like lightnin', it's quite frightenin'.
> But don't be afraid of the dark, in the park,
> not a scream or a cry or a bark, more like a spark.
> You tremble like an alcoholic, muscles tighten up.
> What's that? Lighten up. You see a sight but suddenly
> You feel like you're in a horror flick.

You grab your heart and wish for tomorrow quick.
Music's a clue, when I come you're warned.
Apocalypse Now, when I'm done you're gone.
Haven't you ever heard of a MC murderer?
This is the death penalty, and I'm servin' a death wish.
So come on, step to this mystical idea for a lyrical
    professionist.
Friday the 13th, walking down Elm Street,
you come in my realm you get beat.
This is off-limits, so your visions are blurry.
All you see is the meters of the volume.
Pumpin' lyrics of fury.

I love talking trash like that because before I started making records that was my style. Battle-rap style. Mostly just spitting insults, winding cats up. It was easy for me to tell the rapper in a crazy way how I'll eat him and his rhymes for breakfast. Instead of saying, "Yo, you're not better than me," I would twist it around in some old complicated, prolonged, drop your jaw and forget your girl's name kind of way that would punish them with that screw face. It was fun to do joints like that.

There's a little bit of that talking trash on "Musical Massacre" too:

How could I keep my composure
when all sorts of thoughts fought for exposure?
Release, then veins in the brains increase.
When I let off, make a wish, and blow the smoke off my
    piece.
Unloadin', unfoldin', and the rhymes are exploding.

My favorite line in "Musical Massacre" is "Go manufacture a match, send me after a blast. From the master that has to make a musical massacre." When you're writing and you fall into one of those joints . . . And you're like Ahhhhhhhh! You already know they're gonna be mad at this one.

Follow the Leader was released on July 26, 1988, and sold 500,000 copies in its first week out. We were selling at warp speed because we had a major label promoting and distributing us, and also because now we were on MTV. Back then they played videos all day long, and when they played a video, people from coast to coast saw it, radio stations got behind it, and the album got bigger. We were ignored by a lot of radio stations because we didn't make radio-friendly hits, so MTV was really important for us. It introduced hip-hop and its artists to millions of people. One week after *Follow the Leader* came out, MTV debuted *Yo! MTV Raps*, a show devoted to hip-hop videos and interviews with artists. It started on Saturday nights at 10 p.m. as a half-hour show and quickly became one of MTV's most popular shows. We were on one of the first episodes.

MTV changed the way I wrote music. Videos became such a big part of it all that I started writing songs with lyrics that were more visual. Sometimes I had a video concept in mind, but sometimes I just wanted to make sure people could really see what I was talking about.

What could you say as the earth gets further and further away,
planets as small as balls of clay.
Astray into the Milky Way, world's out of sight.
Far as the eye can see, not even satellites.

Now stop and turn around and look.
As you stare into darkness, your knowledge is took!
So keep starin', soon you suddenly see a star.
You better follow it cause it's the R!

I wanted people to see themselves floating through outer space, but Eric had a different idea and we shot a throwback Al Capone style movie. It wasn't my first vision, but at least I look damn good in a tux.

■ ■ ■

By now, hip-hop, our generation's culture and music, was thriving beyond anything that anyone even a year earlier had imagined. The same year *Follow the Leader* came out, DJ Jazzy Jeff and the Fresh Prince dropped *He's the DJ, I'm the Rapper*. Boogie Down Productions put out *By All Means Necessary*. Run-DMC released *Tougher than Leather*. *A Salt with a Deadly Pepa* by Salt-N-Pepa was released on the same day as *Follow the Leader*. Rob Base and DJ E-Z Rock dropped *It Takes Two*. Slick Rick's *The Great Adventures of Slick Rick*, 2 Live Crew's *Move Somethin'*, N.W.A's *Straight Outta Compton*, and Public Enemy's *It Takes a Nation of Millions to Hold Us Back* all dropped in 1988 too.

During that era artists started realizing that they could sell a lot of records if their song was on the radio all day. On our first albums, we produced the songs and then we picked which one we thought would be the best as the first single. We didn't go into the studio saying, "All right, today we are going to make the single." We went in organically, laid everything down, and then after we were done were like "Yo, this is the one right here."

It was a major turning point in other ways. When we started out, we were making records we loved, which radio *happened* to want to play. And now hip-hop artists began catering to the radio and trying to make pop songs and records solely focused on securing radio play all day. Everybody wanted radio play instead of artists making songs they were passionate about or songs that made a statement or songs that kept it true to hip-hop. Hip-hop lost its way. I knew that opportunity to make more money by catering to radio over my creative impulses existed, but I never wanted to do that. I understood I had a choice. I could try to make a couple of them songs or stay on my path. I never tried. Artists lined up along divides, like pop artists versus underground artists. I chose to stay with the heavy New York City–oriented sound, driven by what we called in those days Motown samples.

Back then it was like you had a repetition of words and then a scratch. Hooks didn't get big until the '90s. In the beginning it was a dope phrase, scratch, horns, whatever, and then back to the rhyme. Compared to three sixteen bars now, in some of my songs the verse was twenty-four, thirty bars, or however long it took me to get my point across. There were no boundaries and no set formats. But as time went on, songs got down to sixteen bars and became hook heavy. Rap evolved from rhyme style into songs. Rap grew, and songs got better.

We started to understand the business side of it a lot more too: knowing how to market yourself, realizing what sells and what doesn't sell, what gets you on the radio in NYC, what gets you on the radio on the West Coast or down south, what gets you big sales overseas. We started realizing it was bigger than just going to the studio.

ENERGY

PART FIVE

Casualties of War

Casualties of war; as I approach the barricade
Where's the enemy, who do I invade?
Bullets of Teflon, bulletproof vest rip
Tear you out of your frame with a bag full of clips
'Cause I got a family that waits for my return
To get back home is my main concern
I'ma get back to New York in one piece
But I'm embedded in the sand that is hot as the city streets
Sky lights up like fireworks blind me
Bullets whistling over my head remind me . . .
President Bush said attack
Flashback to Nam, I might not make it back
Missile hits the area, screams wake me up
from my war of dreams, heat up the M-16.
Basic training, trained for torture.
Take no prisoners, and I just caught cha
Addicted to murder, send more body bags
They can't identify 'em, leave the name tags
I get a rush when I see blood and dead bodies on the floor

Casualties of war
Casualties of war
Casualties of war
Casualties of war
Day divides the night and night divides the day
It's all hard work and no play
More than combat, it's far beyond that
'Cause I got a kill or be killed kind of attack
Areas mapped out, there'll be no Stratego
Me and my platoon make a boom wherever we go
But what are we here for? Who's on the other side of the wall?
Somebody give the president a call
But I hear warfare scream through the air
Back to the battlegrounds, it's war they declare
A Desert Storm: let's see who reigns supreme
Something like Monopoly: a government scheme
Go to the army, be all you can be.
Another dead soldier? Hell no, not me.
So I start letting off ammunition in every direction.
Allah is my only protection.
But wait a minute, Saddam Hussein prays the same.
And this is Asia, from where I came.
I'm on the wrong side, so change the target.
Shooting at the general, and where's the sergeant?
Blame it on John Hardy Hawkins for bringing me to America.
Now its mass hysteria.
I get a rush when I see blood, dead bodies on the floor.
Casualties of war
Casualties of war
Casualties of war

Casualties of war

The war is over, for now at least.

Just because they lost it don't mean it's peace.

It's a long way home, it's a lot to think about.

A whole generation, left in doubt.

Innocent families killed in the midst.

It'll be more dead people after this.

So I'm glad to be alive and walking.

Half of my platoon came home in coffins.

Except the general, buried in the storm

in bits and pieces, no need to look for 'em.

I played it slick and got away with it,

rigged it up so they think that they did it.

Now I'm home on reserves and you can bet

when they call, I'm going AWOL,

'cause it ain't no way I'm going back to war

when I don't know who or what I'm fighting for.

So I wait for terrorists to attack.

Every time a truck backfires I fire back.

I look for shelter when a plane is over me.

Remember Pearl Harbor? New York will be over, G.

Kamikaze, strapped to bombs.

No peace in the East, they want revenge for Saddam.

Did I hear gunshots, or thunder?

No time to wonder, somebody's going under.

Put on my fatigues and my camouflage,

take control, cause I'm in charge.

When I snapped out of it, it was blood and dead bodies on
the floor.

Casualties of war

Casualties of war
Casualties of war
Casualties of war

Notes on "Casualties of War"

I felt like an elder statesman by the time I wrote "Casualties of War," which appeared on our fourth album, *Don't Sweat the Technique*. I knew my audience expected me to be serious on the mic, and as I grew older, keeping it real had to mean more than just talking about the street. I had to go further. "Casualties of War" was a song I did for my friends who went into the US military right out of high school. Teddy Oakes and others fought in Iraq in the Persian Gulf War, which began in August 1990 and lasted through February 1991. I knew these guys pretty well coming up, so when they got home I could see they were different. I could see the war on them. War had changed them. I could see in their eyes that they had been traumatized. They looked hollowed out and vacant and numb. In war you get shot at, you see people you know step on mines and get blown to bits, you kill people, and all of that weighs on you. When you see people strap on bombs and run into crowded buildings, it's going to change how you see things.

I sat down to write and tried to put myself in their boots. I tried to feel the bullets whizzing past my head and the bombs going off. I wanted to feel the fear of being in war. I tried to picture myself going through what they were going through. Like in the first and second verse:

> *Missile hits the area, screams wake me up*
> *from my war dreams, heat up the M-16.*
> *Basic training, trained for torture.*
> *Take no prisoners, and I just caught you.*

I was trying to put myself in the trenches with them. Like really facing death. I had to show the world what they were going through.

"Casualties of War" was what I considered a serious concept song. I wanted to focus on the injustices of the Persian Gulf War. From front to back, no partying in that shit. There's no driving in the Benz down 145th Street. It was all about what was happening on the battlefield and how it was affecting our generation of youth from the hood as well as innocent people in Iraq.

> *I look for shelter when the plane is over me.*
> *Remember Pearl Harbor? New York could be over, G.*
> *Kamikaze, strapped with bombs.*
> *No peace in the East, they want revenge for Saddam.*
> *Did I hear gunshots, or thunder?*
> *No time to wonder, somebody's going under.*

There was also anger in that song, obviously, when I made reference to dead generals killed by friendly fire, as well as references to guys profiting off tragedies like war. My political messages were continuing to evolve by the time I wrote it. As

I was growing older, Martin Luther King Jr.'s and Muhammad Ali's struggles against American injustices were beginning to make more sense. Ali had made similar commentary about the injustice of the United States war in Vietnam: "I ain't got no quarrel with the Vietcong," he told a reporter when he refused to be drafted and inducted into the Armed Forces Examining and Entrance Station. "No Vietcong ever call me a nigger." Dr. King also criticized the US role in Vietnam in his April 4, 1967, speech ("Beyond Vietnam: A Time to Break Silence") at Riverside Church in New York City, exactly a year before his assassination. Despite their critique of Vietnam and mine of Iraq, at the end of the day, power—and in Iraq, oil—prevailed.

When I was younger and closer to the success of my debut album, I would have found it to be dangerous to my career to make such strong statements. But I felt that by my fourth album, I was a bit more settled in my career. As I've said elsewhere, I was inspired in my formative years by people like Minister Malcolm X and President John F. Kenney and Dr. Martin Luther King Jr. One of the things that inspired me was their courage, their willingness to not show fear when standing up for what they believed. I used to look at Martin Luther King, watch his life story. He knew they were going to kill him. He kept doing his thing. Showed no fear. Now, that's courage. Standing at a podium knowing that at any minute these dudes were going to blow your head off—that's pressure. The same thing with Malcolm X. He knew they were going to kill him. And yet he went to the Audubon Ballroom that day and approached the podium, started his day like any other day. And when they ran up on him with the guns out, he looked right at them. That's courage. That's pressure. Folks like this sacrifice for the better of everyone in terms of rights, equality, education, etc. They give their lives. I've always wondered what it takes for a man to be built like that. I feared for them after the fact, watching documentation of what happened to them. That they overcame their fear and pressed on, knowing the dangers, is just incredible to me.

Whenever I made political statements in my music, part of me was channeling the respect I have for these men. To stand on principle, when I'm not even on their scale, made me feel I should have no fear in making those statements. I felt the same way even when my name and the song "Casualties of War" became associated with 9/11 in news stories back in 2001—even though I had published the song nine years earlier. I sat down to write about the Persian Gulf War and its impact and entered the zone. The experience led me to exaggerate the feeling. The result was a song that predicted the World Trade Center attack.

"Casualties of War" was reality in the present and in the future. You can't fault me for telling the truth. I said what I meant, and I meant what I said, and if I wasn't supposed to say it, it wouldn't have ended up on a record.

ENTER THE ZONE

What's intriguing, mystical, and unpredictable about being an artist is that you can't always explain how some things work. But artists know about this certain mood, this zone you can get into where what seems impossible becomes possible. Sometimes it's like the total opposite: you can't write even a phrase that day, let alone a song—and you know it. But when you're in the zone, it's like the ideas and the words wouldn't stop. *You want me to write another one today?* And you know the difference. So you try to lean over to that creative side where things are flowing. You always try to tap into that. And sometimes you tap into that side where it's flowing, but you tap into something where you're getting information that you would normally not have known.

I believe that some of the people who have achieved game-changing, groundbreaking innovations in music have similar stories about pushing themselves to the height of their creativity. They reach a place where all of a sudden not only are you fluent at what you do, but now thoughts are coming to you that you never thought before. And I'm speaking from personal experience. In those moments, answers come to me that I never thought about before and concepts come to me that I never even would have imagined. That's when I feel I am in that zone and I am a vehicle for something greater than I know and understand.

Divine universal consciousness is a source of information that's stored deep in the mind. For the most part, it's almost like everything that exists in the universe is in one place and you can tap into it and get information from it that you may not have known before. I believe a realm of intelligence exists around us; we just have to know how to access it. The place I'm talking about exists. There are things we don't know, but we already know. Here's the perfect example. Long before we're born, before the sperm and egg join, the sperm knows exactly what to do: be the first one to that egg. It knows exactly what to do from the beginning. How does that work? That's nature. It's divine nature. It's divine consciousness.

How to get there? Nobody knows. And ain't nobody supposed to know. Some people meditate to get to this consciousness. It's why people say, "I'm trying to catch the vibe," meaning, they're trying to reach that vibration and frequency where their mind is clicking on all cylinders. When it happens in sports, an athlete says, "I can't explain what happened. I was in the zone, and I just started hitting every shot." Right. They can't really explain it, but it's like they found perfection. It's magic. Can't explain magic, yet people say, "Make magic," or they try to express what happened in the studio as "It was like magic. I came in and everything was just right." A lot of people experience that but don't know what it is. They just think, *Wow my pen was flowing that day.*

Imagine you're playing basketball. You shoot a jump shot,

and you try to shoot the same way every time. You try to jump and land in the same spot every time. You alter your approach to achieve this, so your body has to make adjustments, your mind has to make adjustments, everything has to be in tune—your touch on the ball, your radar to the rim, your mathematical calculations. Everything has to be in synch. That's one of those places you can find yourself sometimes, a moment when everything is in tune, when your body is in tune with your mind. Everything is working at once. You're in this place that is hard to achieve normally, because you're not normally going to hit 50 points every night. And you're not going to write a hit song every time you walk into a studio, or a bestselling book every time you sit down with pen and paper. So when you do get there, you know the stars were aligned. Everything was perfect. You weren't letting anything physical interfere with your mind. Your body did everything perfectly and everything beyond the imaginable. That's bliss. That's tranquility.

Divine universal consciousness is a mystical place that doesn't exist—but it does, and trying to understand it is one of the things that makes artists great. This unknown is what makes us push ourselves to try to be out of this world.

When they say man has no resources to get certain information, and yet he somehow comes up with it mentally, some believe it's because he tapped into the divine consciousness. It's the place people tap into when they're in the zone. Basically, everything you need to know exists in this realm of consciousness. It's shown and proven by people who manage to come up with information they have no ways of getting.

Moses said a bush spoke to him and told him to write the Ten Commandments. The Ten Commandments, when you think about it, are basic principles. At the time, they weren't known, but they were needed. And all of them were solutions to problems. I have to think that the voice Moses heard was in his head. I can imagine him thinking, *What can help make things better where I'm from? We have to change the way people think and act. Okay?* "Thou shalt not steal," "Thou shalt not commit adultery"—these really were nothing out of this world. Somebody just needed to tap into a universal source of knowledge that would be useful for everyone. And for the most part, knowledge is something that empowers people as a whole or does something for the greater good of humanity. This universal source of knowledge is the place where some say Nostradamus came up with his many predictions and where Albert Einstein figured out his concepts on relativity. These people all had to be tapping into a divine source. And the results are just confirmation that it exists.

Not to suggest I wrote the manual to rocket ships, but a lot of the things I came up with in my rhymes were me tapping into something outside myself. To be truthful, I knew what was within my reach, and I would sit down and write a rhyme and come up with things that were beyond my reach. The more you do this again and again, the more you're aware of it, and the more you try to tap into that source of knowledge. I always went to the studio not knowing what I was going to do. But to impress myself means I did something I didn't plan on doing. And to be truthful with myself, I always felt it was something I was tapping into. I used to feel that things were being presented to me. Of course everyone has certain expectations of him or herself when it comes to their area of expertise. Your ego is telling you, *This is what you do.* So you push yourself and you do your thing. But you know what you're capable of regardless of what your ego is telling you, what people say you can do, or what people expect from you. I guess when I exceeded my expectations is when I found myself in the zone, and I got information I felt I normally wouldn't have known. Things came to me that I wouldn't have thought about reaching for.

Whenever I experienced that, I just felt the information was from a higher power, a higher consciousness. It sounds mystic to say, "Yeah, I wrote that, but I didn't write that." But sometimes it's the truth. I know what I'm capable of, and sometimes ideas came to me and it was like *What is this? Why am I thinking of this right now?* And then it makes sense. A good example is when I wrote "Casualties of War."

When I got the track it sounded like war to me. So I started writing the track. I've never been to war, but I started writing the track and the bars just started coming to me. I knew what I was trying to do, but then something starts telling me to say this, say this, mention this. And it just so happened that some of the things I wrote about in my song "Casualties of War" in 1992 actually happened on September 11, 2001, at 8:45 a.m.

On 9/11, I was at home in Connecticut, watching the news on television with live coverage of the World Trade Center towers burning. The phone rang and I answered. It was Al Star, a friend from California.

"Ra, go on the internet."

"For what?"

"Go on the internet."

"Yo, what is going on? I'm watching the news and I can see the World Trade Center on fire."

"Yo, I know, but go on the internet. They are talking about the Twin Towers burning down, and they are posting a quote from you on there."

Back in the day when you went on the internet, there was dial-up. And when you signed on to AOL, all the news popped up: "News of the Day." The first thing that popped up that day was a story about the Twin Towers. Next to that were my photo and a quote from "Casualties of War."

The news story had listed several quotes, including, "'Cause it ain't no way I'm going back to war / when I don't know who or what I'm fighting for." But the main reference from the song was the part where I said those who suffered from the US attacks in Desert Storm were going to come back for revenge and hit the Twin Towers.

> *So I wait for terrorists to attack.*
> *Every time a truck backfires I fire back.*
> *I look for shelter when a plane is over me.*
> *Remember Pearl Harbor? New York will be over, G.*
> *Kamikaze, strapped to bombs,*
> *No peace in the East, they want revenge for Saddam.*
> *Did I hear gunshots, or thunder?*
> *No time to wonder, somebody's going under.*

I wanted to do a song about the casualties of war. I did what I do: I got lost in my work. And when I got into this world of the subject I was writing about, I went deeply into what it would mean to truly be at war. As a writer, you look for anything and everything to write about. But sometimes something hits you like *bang* when you weren't really looking for that. Moments before, you were thinking, *I know how I'm going to approach this. I want to take it to this.* But then something presents itself. It's almost like having a math problem in front of you and you have no idea how to answer it. Then all of a sudden it just starts answering itself in front of you when you know you don't know the answer. That divine source of power will give you information that you have no knowledge of. And this is the only way I can explain how I wrote "Casualties of War" in the way it was written.

In the case of writing rhymes in general, you try to block everything out and focus in on what you're doing. The more focused, inspired, and passionate you are, the greater the possibilities. Setting the room helps set the mood, and that's what you're trying to do. You want to reach that point of creativity where it's just flowing. No distractions, with the room comfortable like you want it. You're trying to get to that place where everything is ten times more exaggerated. You want to get to that level where you're at your highest point for expressing your art. Tap into it.

DIVINE UNIVERSAL CONSCIOUSNESS: FREQUENCIES

When you start to explore a greater understanding of Divine Universal Consciousness, you begin to see patterns in both history and science that tap directly into that shared knowledge. These manifest from a mathematical code that can be witnessed in both the works of nature and the works of man. They are categorized and decoded through theories such as the God Frequency, the Golden Ratio, and what Tesla called the Key to the Universe, but before you begin to decipher these, you need understand a simple principle: music is energy and energy evokes response. When I want to produce a certain response—an emotion like happiness, a thought process such as empathy, or an action like banging your head—I manipulate the energy (or often it manipulates me) through a change in its vibration. That change in vibration is measured in frequency and understanding the mathematics behind those measurements is the science of how I make music.

HIGHER MATHEMATICS

To explain this, I need to take you on a journey that starts with a basic explanation of "higher mathematics" or what some people refer to as "vortex math." This is the concept that numbers are not simply symbols of quantity as we are taught in school, but instead are qualitative entities with interconnected relationships and higher meanings. Very briefly, it categorizes digits into physical (1, 2, 4, 5, 7, 8) and quantum or governing (3, 6, 9). When added together, physical numbers create an interlocking helix ($1 + 1 + 2$, $2 + 2 = 4$, $4 + 4 = 8$, $8 + 8 = 16$ then $1 + 6 = 7$, $7 + 7 = 14$ then $1 + 4 = 5$, $5 + 5 = 10$ then $1 + 0 = 1$ and the loop repeats). This represents the natural flow of energy. The quantum numbers three and six have both a linear connection ($3 + 3 = 6$, $6 + 6 = 12$ then $1 + 2 = 3$, repeat) and a "governing" connection to the physical numbers (of which any combination adds up to a quantum number). The number nine is an entity unto itself, as each of its multiples equal 9 and arguably exists on an even higher plane in relation to the other governing numbers ($3 + 6 = 9$, $3 \times 3 = 9$, $6 \times 6 = 36$ then 9, $3 \times 6 = 18$ then 9, etc.). Together, quantum numbers govern the flow of energy while the number nine either oversees all or oversees nothing.

It's easy to dismiss this as an interesting but inconsequential piece of arithmetical coincidence, but in the physical universe, these patterns and loops continuously seem to appear in nature and science. From the basic helix of DNA to the dissection of a circle's radius (360, 180, 90, 45) and the honeycombs created by bees, the presence of vortex math and in particular the number 9 can often be interpreted. Both the Earth's electromagnetic field and the alpha frequency of a human brain at rest are documented to be 7.83 Hz (7 + 8 + 3 = 18). The Golden Ratio, another concept of "higher mathematics" found throughout natural forms, can be rounded to 1.62. The most typical representation of vortex numbers—a circle dissected by a triangle of 9, 6, 3 with a geometric helix representing the energy flow of the physical numbers—is perfectly aligned with the architecture of the Pyramids, an ancient wonder that has always captured my imagination and, as with anything that inspires me, a significant amount of my time researching it.

There are volumes of documentation and speculation surrounding the creation, true purpose, and powers of the Pyramids of Giza and the Great Pyramid in particular. I've probably read most of it. Their placement, dimensions, and construct adhere to geometric, astrological, and sound frequency theories that were not formally proposed or recorded until centuries or even millennia after their completion. This suggests a knowledge and consciousness in the builders that can be described as divine, but what's always captured my imagination most vividly is the way references to higher mathematics, pitch, and tonality seem hidden in plain sight throughout their architecture and aesthetics. Inside the Grand Gallery are seven corbelled stone steps and above the Kings Chamber are five granite beams serving as chamber dividers just like the seven white keys and five black keys on the musical scale of a piano. The two ramps leading out Grand Gallery are each cut vertically with twenty-seven notches. These fifty-four notches when doubled equal 108 then 216 then 432. The dimensions and materials of the Kings Chamber are notable for creating an incredible resonance that adheres to a frequency of 54 Hz, but also a reference pitch of 432 Hz. The adjacent pyramids within the

Giza Complex are placed according to Phi, the Golden Ratio, and theoretically would amplify the Great Periods pitch to 432 Hz. It is easy to picture the great monument as the world's most formidable tuning fork.

GOD FREQUENCY

The frequency 432 Hz is often referred to as the God Frequency. Prior to an international board of standards arbitrarily setting the Standard A note at 440 Hz in 1940, it was the nexus frequency used in classical compositions by Verdi and many others. 432 Hz resonates with the previously mentioned electromagnetic field of the Earth (7.83 Hz—the Schumann Resonance or the "Earths heartbeat") and aligns with the Golden Ration of Phi. It was championed by Tesla as the key to unlocking the energy of the universe, and, experientially, it is said to connect a listener both emotionally and physically with nature and the solar system. Some scientists go further to proclaim its healing properties down to the cellular level. What I can say without hesitation is 432 Hz sounds better to me. When I listen to music that is played at 440 Hz A tuning, it feels more aggressive and disconnecting. It evokes a different physiological response. In some cases, aggression may be the intended response. And in other cases, you may want to feel love or sadness. Whenever I'm creating music, my first step is always to get the feel for the different vibrational frequencies. When I was really young, I never thought about this very deeply, but as my technique matured, it became important to match my words with the feelings created by the music in a more specific way. Most recording software has meters built in to measure this so you can get very precise with this process, but more often than not, my ear and my energy are in tune and I just put a track on and vibe out.

I'm personally convinced that the higher mathematics behind frequencies plays a significant role in the physical, emotional, and spiritual responses to the energy of musical vibrations. I also believe connections between the frequencies that occur in nature and the repeated application of the same ratios in man-made monuments, manuscripts, and other works of art throughout history are the result of the shared knowledge of Divine Universal Consciousness. Regardless of what your personal research may lead you to conclude about the origins and spirituality of higher mathematics and conscious connectivity, if you can accept the core principle that music is vibration, vibration is energy, and energy evokes response, you can begin to focus your creative process. If you can accept that energy exists within yourself and you have an inherent, internal knowledge from which to draw, you will never be without inspiration. There is no doubt that a lot of the stories I shape, the words I choose, the rhymes I write, and the music I create are born of the observations and experiences of the world around me. But sometimes a walk down the streets of New York, time spent staring at the stars, the music I listen to, or the guidance of my idols don't ignite my pen. It's at these times, I have the confidence as an artist to look within, knowing that the spark needed is always smoldering inside and I can build the fire all by myself.

WHO'S GONNA
TAKE THE WEIGHT?

Back in mid-1988, just as the *Follow the Leader* album was coming out, we headlined the Dope Jam Tour, with my big brother Kool Moe Dee opening up, along with my old friend Biz Markie. Back in the day, he used to come by my high school and beat-box. It was a great feeling to pull up to the venue and see my name on the marquee. We got $30,000 a night.

When we were in London getting ready to do a show for the tour, I found out my grandmother's funeral was the following day. She had died days earlier, but my family had kept it from me because they didn't want me to cancel my shows and fly home. They called me when they felt it was too late for me to make the services, thinking I wouldn't ruin my plans. But I jumped on the next plane I could get home anyway. I got in a little trouble for canceling several shows at the last moment—if you develop a reputation for canceling shows it'll kill your touring career. Of course I wouldn't for the world miss saying goodbye to my grandmother—she was incredibly important—but it also meant a lot of people on my team didn't get paid when they'd expected to. My career meant a lot of people depended on me for work. I felt like many people were standing on my shoulders, and it was a lot of weight. I had a career, and my career had me. And, of course, the fans were important to me.

A few months later I got a call saying Felicia was going into labor, several days earlier than we'd expected and just an hour before another show. I'd planned to be home by the due date so we could welcome the baby together, but instead I was in Tennessee. I was eighteen and so overwhelmed by the machine pushing my career along and all the people who relied on me that I didn't feel like I could cancel a show again. Which felt crazy. Did I have the wrong priorities? What was I doing?

After the show I flew back home and held my son, Tahmell. He was the most beautiful thing I had ever seen. When I got back in the studio, I thought, *One day Tahmell will listen to my music. I want to write things that will impress him.* I went back out on the road when he was a week old. Now Felicia was working hard at home with the baby while I was doing shows and then going out to bars with my crew. When she called, we argued a lot. Almost broke up. I had to try to understand the new reality she was going through as a mother. Her life had changed a lot more than mine had.

Felicia had always stood by me, and it hurt to not be there for her. When Felicia was near the end of her senior year in high school, and I was back home from touring, we went to Dapper Dan's in Harlem to plan our outfits for her prom. That was the ultimate star trip. Dap was the original hip-hop clothing designer. He took fabric from any major label and remade it into anything you wanted—a suit, a hat, a dress, a car seat, whatever. Suddenly you had the Gucci and Louis Vuitton labels all over lots of things they hadn't made. They said Dap was stealing, but I said he was sampling. Just like I was making new records out of bits of old records, he was making clothes out of clothes. He was my man, and he designed a lot of my favorite stuff back then that I rocked on album covers and onstage.

Felicia and I picked out matching Fendi outfits in brown and rust, the original Fendi colors. She had a dress with a little jacket, and I had a suit. Dap was gonna put Fendi fabric on these Timberlands I had and make the whole outfit come together. When Felicia and I showed up in Dapper Dan outfits, everyone would be talking about us.

But on the day of the prom, I went to Dap's to pick up the outfits and he said he was really sorry but they weren't ready. He needed one more day. I closed my eyes and tried to keep from yelling at him. Somehow I chilled, but he had screwed up my girl's prom.

I went back to Felicia and said I had bad news. She just slumped into the couch, so sad and disappointed. It was heartbreaking for me to think I had allowed this happen to her. I told her I would run out and get us new outfits, I was ready to scramble, but she said no. "Let's not go." The sound of her saying that was like a dagger in my heart. That was her big moment, and I felt like I'd let her down. She forgave me, but I never forgot it.

Touring also kept me away from my father when he needed me most. Six months after my first child was born I was on tour when my father started to get really sick. Bone cancer was eating him up. I wanted to be with him all the time, but I was out on the road. I'd already postponed a bunch of shows after my grandmother's funeral, and I didn't think I could just leave the tour again. Plus, I thought my father would be okay. That's because my family wasn't telling me how bad he was.

I was only weeks away from my first trip to Africa—we had shows coming up in Senegal and Nigeria—when Ronnie called. My father had died. It was 1989. I just collapsed onto the bed and didn't move for hours. I went to the funeral but in the days that followed I felt paralyzed in my soul. I didn't care what it cost. I couldn't go on tour.

For weeks I sat in the crib and played just two things: Miles Davis's "Bitches Brew" and Bob James's "Nautilus." They were heavy, moody, otherworldly, and the only songs that made sense to me. I played them over and over and just let them take over my mood. It was eating at me that I hadn't been there for Pops when he was sick because I'd been on tour. Thanks to hip-hop I had become my own man, free to travel the world as I pleased, without a boss ever telling me no. But now I also felt like I was trapped in my career like it was a golden prison. Anyone would envy being in there, except you couldn't have time off to actually be there for your family.

Pop's death took the air out of me. I didn't want to write rhymes anymore. I didn't even want to hear hip-hop. I was done. For months I didn't write a rhyme or touch a mic. I couldn't even set foot in the studio. I just sat on the couch and zoned out. I wasn't in my own body.

After six months, I met a producer named Paul C who played me a beat that really moved me. It was a loop from the funk band 24-Carat Black's album *Ghetto: Misfortune's Wealth*, and it just hit a nerve. It sounded like a beat my father would have liked. It gave me a sense of reality being cold and harsh, which was exactly how I was feeling at the time. I knew I could use that beat to say something about my father, and that made me want to write again. I took that loop and played it over and over, and then I wrote "In the Ghetto." Making that record released a lot of my pain and helped me remember how much I loved making music. It reminded me that making records was a worthwhile way to spend my life, and it made me want to get back to it. I knew Pops would've wanted me to get back to work.

When I went into my third album, *Let the Rhythm Hit 'Em*, I was one of the biggest names in the game, and no one was going to take my spot. There had to be something I could do better or some way I could be better. I had to go further and deeper. I had to take my songs to the next level. The only challenge to my throne was complacency.

■ ■ ■

For years I'd been getting on a plane almost every other day even though I knew how fragile these machines really were. I'd seen how complex the inner workings of planes were and how much all the mechanics in my father's shop had needed him to help fix major problems. What about all the shops that didn't have guys that smart? How many planes were being overseen by guys who didn't really know what they were doing? Also, I knew just how much pressure the shops were under to turn around inspections on time to keep the airlines on schedule. Since I was flying all the time, the odds of eventually getting on a plane that wasn't fixed properly seemed pretty high. Was I heading toward dying in a plane crash? "I'm done with planes," I told my manager. "Don't put me on no more planes. If we can't drive there, then don't book the show." He said we could cancel most of our flights and get a tour bus, but there were just a few more shows and it made sense to fly to them. Begrudgingly, I said okay, even as I thought, *A plane is a big, heavy metal tube racing through the air. How can that succeed every single time?*

A few weeks later we were up in the air and I was in first class while my whole crew was in coach. When they said we could get up and move around I went back and sat with my guys. I was in the last row, sitting in the aisle seat, when the plane just dropped like we'd gone over a cliff. We had hit an air pocket and bounced down so rapidly that the liquid from my drink came up out of my cup and rose into the air, then splashed down onto my pants. People were screaming. I looked at my manager like, *I told you I didn't want to fly anymore.* He looked scared out of his mind.

After we landed, I told him to cancel all of our upcoming flights. I didn't care. We would travel by bus from now on, period. He said we had six shows coming up in Japan, $100,000 each. *Damn, I gotta fly one last time.* Flying to Tokyo was seventeen stressful hours in the grip of anxiety. You wouldn't have known it by looking at me, because on the outside I was as cool as the other side of the pillow. But inside I was in hell. I had visions of the guts of the plane falling out because some guy in the shop had missed something. The whole time I felt like we were about to die.

We landed safely, praise Allah.

In Tokyo, when people came up, I didn't understand them, but I noticed they all used the same word. I didn't know what they were talking about, but I heard that word again and again. Finally a girl told me they were calling me "the master." A master of hip-hop. At my shows people were rhyming every word of my songs even though they knew no English at all. It blew my mind to see that I could connect to people through music even if they didn't speak my language.

The night before we flew home, I had a dream where the plane started coming apart as we were in flight. I woke up in the middle of the night and I said, *Okay this is really, really, really the last time I'm ever getting on a plane.*

The tour bus life was much nicer. I'd spend rides moving around the cabin or looking out the window and watching the country go by. Being on the ground was relaxing. Now we were going at a speed where I could look around and take everything in, as opposed to traveling at a blur, which made me feel like my life was slipping away. On the bus, I had a chance to think and let my mind flow into new territory. Being on the open road helped me feel gassed up as an artist and let me enjoy touring again.

END OF AN ERA

Hollywood was starting to call, and it was pissing me off. In 1991 and 1992 a lot of hip-hop movies were being made, like *Boyz n the Hood* and *New Jack City*, and a lot of the producers behind those movies asked me to audition. But for some reason they always asked me to be a drug dealer or a gangster or some sort of gun toter. It was the only thing Hollywood thought I could do. The producers of *CB4* offered me a role as a stickup man. The producers of *Juice* tossed me a negative part too. At least eight other films called. It got so offensive that an offer would come in and I wouldn't even get the name of the movie.

"We have an offer for you to be in a movie," my manager would say.

"What do they want me to do?"

"They want you to play a thug who—"

"Nope."

Why were they always asking me to be a stereotypical gun-totting, drug-dealing, murderous gangster onscreen? No, thank you. Sure, it's kind of well known I got arrested for my first gun charge at age twelve, but that's not something I thought defined who I was as a man, and I certainly I wasn't going to advertise it. I didn't rhyme about guns much, I didn't make them part of my videos, and I wasn't about to promote them on an even bigger screen. Did I look like a drug dealer to them? I had big dookie chains, sweatsuits, and Benzos. That's how drug dealers looked in the late '80s and '90s, but it's also how a lot of regular people in the streets were dressing. It wasn't a costume. I was a successful recording artist, and I had money. So when I bought a chain, I spent $10,000. Maybe a drug dealer would too. But the similarities stopped there. So I guess when I dressed like the street in my income bracket, I looked like a drug dealer. To a Hollywood producer or a middle American theatre-goer, that was really more their perception than my reality. But I think some people were going to see me like that no matter what. I turned down all requests to play a drug dealer without blinking. Don't get me wrong, some of my best friends are drug dealers, but I'm not playing that onscreen.

Only once did I make an exception.

Jam Master Jay came by the crib one night holding a script he'd written. "Ra, I know you don't play drug dealers," he said, "but I wrote this character with you in mind."

I knew Jay wasn't stereotyping me. He overstood me, respected me, and wanted great things for my career. He explained how he saw there was a difference between an artist playing a part and a human being defined as a stereotype. So I was willing to consider it for him. He said it was a drug dealer, but it would remind me of people we knew. He said it was art, and he needed me to ride with him on this. He said I could trust him. He'd never make me look bad.

Jay was my brother. For him, I was willing to break my rule.

"Okay, man. I'll do it for you."

We toasted, excited we were finally going to work together. But the start of the movie got delayed, and we never found time to reschedule. He did change my viewpoint that night, though. But even with my new outlook, I still wasn't finding roles in movies that had a message I could support. But I loved the movies and thought there had to be a way I could contribute to the artform. I started attending prescreenings and other events—for movies like *Juice*, starring Tupac Shakur.

The movie was about four Harlem teens facing adversity from all sides and within. Right after I saw the film, the director, Ernest Dickerson, said he wanted me to write the lead song for the soundtrack. He told me to put the spirit of the movie into a song. I ran home to my studio and grabbed a stack of records I'd put aside. The record on top was Nat Adderley's "Rise, Sally, Rise." I didn't need to look any further. I put it on and I thought about what can happen when you go after things the fast way. I thought about what juice means in the hood and how chasing it is dangerous. No matter how hard you are, some days the dice won't fall your way. The street is heartless. It'll eat the ones who love it the most and not think twice—just as Bishop (Tupac's character) got thrown off a roof at the end of the flick. I boiled the whole song down to that part. I created a character based on Bishop who I could put through the streets and show people that surviving in the hood means you have to know everything and see around corners, and even if you do, no matter what, you won't survive.

I still remember the day Tupac was killed. I was at home in Connecticut when the phone rang. "Tupac got shot." Everything in my universe stopped. It hurt at the base of my heart like a member of my family had been shot. In may ways, the movie was a hip-hop tragedy because his death came out of the rules of a segment of society documented through our music, and often personified by hip-hop artists and fans: a real man rules himself, the toughest run the streets, and if the streets knock you down, you've gotta come back ten times harder. That's the code of the streets that birthed and raised hip-hop and one that had become dangerously real with the stratospheric rise of hyper-reality "gangster rap." My life outside of the booth and off the stage definitely had elements of that code, but my music and lyrics, with few exceptions, hadn't been particularly violent in content. I knew moving further from aggression and gangsterism and even closer to cultural and spiritual uplift was where my path was taking me. On each album we released as Eric B. & Rakim, I had purposely introduced more frequent and less subtle references to the lessons and knowledge that inspired me. I was ready to open this door even more.

But in the spring of 1992, as we made *Don't Sweat the Technique,* the world of hip-hop was changing rapidly. I was at home watching TV when my brother called and told me to turn on the news. I flipped to CNN and saw a man in the streets of LA get hit in the face with a brick. I thought I was watching a movie. What the news was calling the Los Angeles riots was the upheaval in the streets from frustration—fighting, looting, tear gas—and it was televised. The whole country watched live. The powder keg had been lit about a year earlier when a slew of cops beat down a black man named Rodney King. They hit him with sticks over and over and kicked him, looking like a gang attacking a rival. Meanwhile, someone in the distance videotaped the whole scene. It was the first time a regular person's videotape became a national news phenomenon. Everyone in the US saw that video and the brutality of those cops. But the jury let them off. That's when South Central LA exploded.

The LA riots went on for five days. I sat at home watching CNN and rooting for the guys in the streets who were tired of living under the heel of the system and finding the courage to stand up. It was a rebellion against injustice—not only the case of Rodney King, but the ongoing police brutality and civil rights violations by police that had become normalized. The anger had been building for decades. And I knew the people rebelling were my people. They were hip-hop. I felt their pain and I stood with them. It felt good to see people stand up and say, "We ain't having it no more."

After the LA riots, the most important MCs in the game were LA rappers, like Snoop, Dr. Dre, and Ice Cube. Their music seemed to come directly out of the environment and the energy that had led to the riots, and it seemed to take on a deeper significance for the nation that was again contemplating the crisis facing a neglected segment of society.

■ ■ ■

Alongside these concerns about the state of hip-hop and the nation, I was facing a personal potential upheaval with Eric B., as we approached the largest clash of intentions since we met six years prior. In 1992, MCA had three options left on our contract. By the time we wrote, recorded, released, and promoted each of those remaining albums, including what would probably be three world tours, it could take us five years or more before we were ready for a new deal. But Eric had an idea to get around that. If he and I both did solo albums and then returned for a final group album, we could be looking at signing a new multimillion dollar contract in less than two years. I signed the paperwork that freed up Eric to do his solo joint.

Within a few months, Eric was ready to submit his project. He called me up and asked me to go with him to see Ernie Singleton, the president of MCA. I wanted to go up to the label anyway and hadn't heard any of his music yet so I was curious. We met up and together went into the meeting. Eric popped in his tape. From where I sat, it didn't go that great. They wanted him to keep working in the studio and it was almost as if they seemed surprised I wasn't part of his project. Singleton even asked, "What did Rakim do?" I thought they understood the whole point was for us to be working independently of each other.

Regardless of the outcome of Eric's meeting on his solo project, I had been waiting long enough to work separate from Eric and was eager to get started. I took the concepts I was building and started reaching out to producers. But there was a problem with the contract. Even though we had agreed to do the two solo albums, the way the options worked meant MCA was only releasing the budgets one at a time. Either Eric needed to sign off that he was done with his project and I could start using the money that was left or MCA needed to accept his record as is, execute the next option, and give me a whole new bag of cash to work with. A couple weeks turned into a couple of months, and it was becoming obvious that neither one of those things was happening.

The label took a hard stance and kept throwing it back at Eric saying until he cleared things up, no money was getting released to me. At the same time, all of a sudden it became real hard for me to reach Eric. I couldn't move forward with my album, I wasn't doing any shows and months kept passing by with nothing going in the bank.

"I can't get paid because I can't find Eric B.," I finally had to tell my wife. Felicia didn't understand that—and to be honest, neither did I. The devil on my shoulder started talking real grimy, but no matter how much my imagination ran away with me, no matter how frustrating Eric was being, no matter how mad he made me, no matter how much the whole situation felt like he was screwing me over, he was still my brother and I needed to see him face-to-face.

I drove out to Eric's place in New Jersey, and some kid opened the door with the chain on and peeked at me through a sliver.

He said, "He ain't here, man." I could tell he was scared.

I said, "Open the door now, kid!"

He just stood there with the chain on the latch, unsure what to do.

I kicked in the door. Took it right off the chain with one hard whack. Eric wasn't there, but two minutes later I finally had him on the phone.

"E., I can't do anything without my money. When are we gonna deal with our business?"

He either couldn't or wouldn't give me an answer. The big plan of getting a lot of music out quick and setting up another huge deal had backfired. I accepted that sometimes things go like that, but I couldn't accept that he seemed to refuse to acknowledge he played any part in it or how his actions and inactions were affecting me. Before that, I never even considered that I wouldn't get back with Eric no matter how big of a success or failure either of our solo projects were, but now I realized he was on his own path. Maybe he always was. I started my solo career the following day.

I got $1 million for my deal by myself, and I, finally, finally, got to be my own man, totally in charge of my destiny. Eric B. & Rakim took a very long pause, and I got to work on the first project in this new chapter of my life.

But the climate of hip-hop had changed. The gangsta content coming out of LA had made such an impact on the charts that now the A&Rs and the artists who followed them seemed to only want to rap about the violence in the streets and the drug economy that fueled it. You had to ask yourself how it was possible that every rapper out could be a former or current narcotics kingpin or gang leader with multiple bodies on their belt, but that's what the new fan base of hip-hop was demanding. When I first started releasing records, most of the fans were urban Black men who listened to the music to ingest creativity and escape from violent reality a lot of them faced. They concentrated on dope beats, the best rhyme skills, and a little bit of intellectualism, but most of all being the flyest brother on the scene. In the gangsta era, a lot of fans, including a good number of new white teenage boys from the suburbs, just wanted a tour through the hardest stories from the hood, and, as sales skyrocketed, that's what the labels gave them. I was ready to push forward with an increasingly conscious message and intricate technique, but the Golden Era of hip-hop with its diversity of style, content, and creativity had come screeching to a halt.

NO OMEGA

Eric B. & Rakim's four albums overlapped perfectly with the Golden Era of hip-hop, from 1986 to 1992. After we ended our partnership, I was tempted to follow what everyone else was doing. Gangsta was the only type of hip-hop that was really selling at that point, so the industry was pressuring all the rappers to be more like that. I could've told gangster stories better than anyone. I could've rhymed about things my friends did in the streets. There were plenty of stories I'd seen and heard. But I'd spent years building myself up as a conscious person who spoke about self-esteem and righteousness. Becoming a gangsta artist would've contradicted all of that. I didn't want to go that route.

. . .

In 1997, I finally felt it was time to start working on my fifth album.

Universal Records gave me an advance of $700,000, less than the previous album, but that meant I'd get less pressure from the label to make pop radio records. The stress I'd been under poured out of me, and I came up with tons of raw, hardcore rhymes. It led me to really push myself. I called that album *The 18th Letter*.

Fans expected a certain style from Rakim, which was totally opposite from the gangsta rap that was going on. The haters and nonbelievers had a reason to get back in my ear, and I had to listen. But deep down all it did was make me want to win. I had to prove them wrong again. People were spiteful, cynical. Not everybody was a fan or supportive of what I wanted to do. People I least expected would've loved to see me fall on my face for whatever reason, sometimes selfish reasons.

I buckled down, focused on what I was doing, and sharpened my steel immediately. It was not like I could sit there and do five tracks and say, "Okay, I got something," and play the best song. A&R were now right there in the studio and I had to give them heat on the first one. "The 18th Letter (Always and Forever)" was the first single, produced by Father Shaheed. As I have always trusted the vibrations of the music, I let the song tell me what to write. I remember getting the confirmation from the label, like "Yeah, that right there is dope. This whole album is going to be dope." It was still an uphill climb because I hadn't been in the studio for so long, but I knew my only competition was myself. I would push to be better than me, and me alone.

"The 18th Letter (Always and Forever)" is one of my favorite joints on the album and one of my favorite songs period. It's a song that explains who I am and what I like to do, and what I'm about. I went basically from rapping about how dope I was from a street point of view to rapping about how dope I was in an overall and more conscious point of view. At this time I was really feeling myself. I was embracing the persona of Rakim being the God

MC. I was trying to say that I had been here at the beginning of time. When I first heard the song, I just started seeing pyramids and obelisks and statues and hieroglyphics and shiny gold, kings and thousands of people in front of a temple saluting. I wanted it to sound like "The king is here!" I felt that song showed me greatness when I envisioned the track, so I tried to express that with what I was saying. In rhyming "Just when things seemed the same, and the whole scene is lame," I was basically saying that the time I was off was beneficial for me but detrimental for other MCs. Even though I'd been gone, the entire time I hadn't missed anything, and actually the game had suffered because I wasn't there.

> *Just when things seemed the same, and the whole scene*
> *is lame*
> *I come in and reign with the unexplained for the brain till*
> *things change.*
> *They strain the sling slang. I'm trained to bring game.*
> *History that I arranged been regained by King James.*

My fans knew who I was and expected the God MC at that point, so I ran with it and tried to take it to the next level. The producers I had on the album were a great help, including Clark Kent, Premier, and Pete Rock. I needed the sound I'm synonymous with. I had to stick to that Rakim sound. Clark Kent is one of the cats who could deliver that all the time. He knows what it is. That's one of my aces in the hole. Clark made it plain: "Ra, this what you supposed to be rhyming to right now." I love Clark's energy. Just the confidence in what he does and the way he feels about his music made me feel the same way. You need somebody like that to keep you excited about what you're doing and somebody who can also bring extra energy to the table.

Hip-hop's sound was now full radio-blown music. It was important for me to not try to fit in with that. I needed a sound that would allow me to keep my integrity and keep my fans, and Clark, Primo, and Pete Rock got that I wasn't trying to change those elements that were at the core of why I was loved and admired as an MC.

I remember getting the track for "It's Been a Long Time" from Primo and hearing the horns, which were like that really hard *baaaadint!!!* I loved the dramatic music, like something was about to happen, that "somebody's coming" type of sound—some triumphant entrance or epic event. As soon as I heard it, I knew it was going to be special. Then, as I'm listening to it, it made me wonder why he hadn't put the rest of the sample in there. He called me up the next day.

"Yo, how do you like the track?" he asked.

I didn't want to say nothing, because you don't question Premier. He knows what he's doing. He's that dude. But I was so anxious to hear the other half of the sample. And it was killing me. "Preme, why didn't you put the other half of the sample in it?"

He started laughing, almost a growling laugh. "You know, the way the song is I had to catch it the way it's on there, but you know, I can try—"

"No, if that's what it is, man, I know it's for a reason. I was just kind of curious to know if there was another half of the sample and what it would sound like. I love the track."

About four months later, I went shopping and bought some records and came home. I'd picked up the record *Call Me*, by Al Green. I put my new vinyl on and heard Al Green and those horns in that call and response: *ba-dant,* "Call me," *ba-dant,* "Call me," *ba-dant,* "Call me." That's why he didn't put in the other piece of the sample: because there's singing through the whole thing. But I picked up the needle and played it again, thinking, *Premier's a genius, man.* Most people would have heard that record and not sampled it, because as soon as you try, the singing starts. For years nobody touched it, probably because of that. And here goes Primo. That's my dude, man. Incredible, incredible. That song kind of let people know I'd been gone for a while: "It's Been a Long Time." Just finding ways to bridge the gap and counteract it.

The album also had "The Saga Begins" and a couple other songs dealing with how long I'd been gone, like "Guess Who's Back." And of course Clark Kent said, "Got to let them know you back." He had everything going perfectly in that song, including the hook sampled from Chuck D: "Once again back is the incredible." Like, who can't come up with something to rhyme with that?

It was a good project, and when it came out, it went gold almost right away. Number one on *Billboard.* I didn't sell ten million albums, but I managed to boost my brand up another couple of notches and just solidify my status as one of the premier lyricists of hip-hop.

THE MASTER AND DR. DRE

When I started doing my sixth album, I thought of the people in Japan who'd called me "the master" and how there were people around the world who understood that I was an expert at this. So

I simply named my album *The Master*. I knew I was still one of the best MCs in the game, but I got an advance of just $300,000. I got the message. I was an older guy in a young man's game, and I wasn't doing radio-friendly songs or even trying to cross over. That meant a smaller budget and a lower risk. I couldn't blame them, and ultimately *The Master* sold less any of my other works, but I'm proud of it and still rock tracks like "The R" and "Flow Forever" to this day.

Meanwhile, DreamWorks Records was struggling, despite having George Michael and a huge war chest. They thought they could revitalize my career, and I liked their energy. Like Lazarus, I was back, getting another deal and joining a company with great vision. We were close to finishing the paperwork when someone at DreamWorks called Dr. Dre to ask if he'd produce some tracks for my album after I signed. Dre said, "After he signs?" He hung up and called me. He said, "Don't sign with them. Come sign with me at Aftermath." Aftermath Entertainment, Dr. Dre's company, offered me just over a million dollars. I said, "Hell yes."

Dr. Dre is one of, if not the greatest producers in hip-hop history. He helped create the sound that dominated West Coast hip-hop, that Parliament-Funkadelic bounce. He produced iconic records for historic MCs like Eazy-E, Ice Cube, Snoop Dogg, and Tupac, and he was working with future greats like 50 Cent and Eminem. This changed everything. Now I had the best musical partner in the game. With Dre beats under me I knew we were going to make a classic.

Dre called and said, "Ra, let's make a dope album. I'm gonna go big with the production. I wanna bring in orchestras and live musicians and create a big sound." He said we'd get started really soon, he just had to finish the album he was doing and then it was on.

I left my three kids with my mom and drove to California with Felicia. She and I did twelve-hour shifts, and I couldn't drive fast enough. After we each did one shift, we were in Oklahoma City. We stopped for dinner, had a good night's sleep, and after two more shifts we were in LA, where Aftermath had a nice apartment set up for us.

I planned to spend three months in LA, but when I started going to Dre's studio, I found out that before he could get to me he actually had to finish two albums—with West Coast rappers Truth Hurts and Xzibit. Six months in, I hadn't really started working with Dre. Of course I was staying active with the pen. I'm a writer and I gotta be writing all the time, so I was going to the studio every night, writing and recording on other producers' beats, but I was holding back my best rhymes for the sessions face to face with Dre. I saw him every now and then, and he'd be like "Ra, I'm about to finish this joint! You're up next! Get ready!" I stayed because I still dreamed of making a classic, but I accepted that it was going to take much longer than I originally expected, so I brought my kids out and set them up in school. I thought, *I've come this far, I've gotta make this work out.* Dre brought in a stack of records and played them to get ideas for samples. He said they sounded cool and he'd build some loops from them, but he didn't.

After a year of waiting to start going 24/7 with Dre, I got really frustrated. I complained, and he gave me a little face time. We sat in the studio and listened to some beats, and he gave me directions on what to rhyme about on the tracks. Almost every time he'd say, "Talk shit on this one." He meant gangsta rap. Dre and

I had a common friend, so he had heard a lot of stories about me and my crew and that is what he wanted me to rhyme about. It was tough to fault him for it initially. It was the content that had driven so many of the classic albums he produced and made him millions of dollars along the way. Now he had a chance to do it with one of the most highly praised lyricists in the game and it wasn't a stretch for him to assume I had some of those types of stories in my bag. All he had to do was turn to the photo on the back cover of *Paid In Full* and see a posse that included "the real" 50 Cent, the man his new artist had taken his name from, and conclude where I came from wasn't all gossip, hype, or folklore.

Dre wanted me to make a record about that, but I wasn't going to do it. That wasn't who I wanted to be. I knew that we could've made the illest gangsta album ever, and it would've been a huge seller, but I was a father of three in my forties. I needed to do more with the mic than tell street stories. I wanted to expand consciously.

After almost three years in LA I still hadn't gotten a beat from Dre that I was really excited about. I made fifteen songs with Aftermath Entertainment, and I used over $300,000 in studio time, but Dre and I had made nothing that I thought reflected who I was as an artist.

Dre was a perfectionist. Dre was busy. But I wondered if part of the impasse was that after so much success Dre couldn't risk a failure and gangsta rap was always a sure thing for him.

I told Dre I was leaving. He said, "Give me a little more time." He wasn't ready to quit. He even offered me $250,000 to stay, but I couldn't do it. He understood and was really cool about it—he said I could keep the songs I'd made, and we shook hands.

I drove back to New York with the family. Things hadn't worked out, but I felt like I'd survived a test. Like others before him, Dr. Dre had tried to change me into something I didn't want to be, and again I was strong enough to say no to a legend. Once again the universe had asked me, *What's more important to you, money or integrity?* I made choices based on what I believed in, and even when there was a lot of money to be made, I stuck to my principles.

■ ■ ■

Back on the East Coast, I settled in with my family and started to plan what was next. The three years I spent in California were not a total waste. I'd reaffirmed that I needed to follow my own path. I'd seen from the inside how you can build not just a successful career but also a successful corporation in the entertainment industry. I was going to invest in myself and one of the first things I did was run out and buy six figures worth of recording equipment, set up a "Rakim only" studio close to home, and start to work with some of my favorite New York producers. Mainstream or underground, I was only going to choose those who understood my vision and would help me be better than myself. Even when I split from Eric and thought I had freedom, I was always somewhat reliant on the industry. Now, I had no contracts and no one to report to on any level. I was the CEO.

But I was also the brand, the product, and the operation all rolled into one. It was solely on me to create the next album completely under my own direction, and I had a major hurdle to overcome. Since my first album, I had executed my creative vision almost as if I was writing an ever evolving book. One chapter set up the next, and the themes and characters developed over the pages. I couldn't escape that I had left a major chapter on the editing room floor in Los Angeles, and I wasn't sure how to just skip ahead without my fans completely losing the plot. Each beat speaks to me vibrationally and each one calls for a different story, so it wasn't as simple as recycling those rhymes into a remix. I needed a premise that would wipe the slate clean, take the best of what had come before, but build a new story. I needed both an apocalypse and a revelation.

The themes behind *The Seventh Seal*, my seventh album released in 2009, were built on those needs and my own vision of what I wanted my art form to inspire. I wanted to break down hip-hop and bring it back to the core themes of love, struggle, and pride. I pushed myself to once again develop new rhyming patterns and injected even more spiritual references than I had before. I also approached the business side in a new manner for myself. Instead of turning an album into a major label, I stayed independent and struck a fifty-fifty joint venture deal for the release—a model commonplace today but still outside of the norm in the mid-2000s. For an independent release, it sold successfully charting at number two its first week, only behind 50 Cent, an artist at the peak of popularity backed by the major label behemoth of Interscope/Universal. I'm immensely proud of both its content and its performance. Following the release, I embarked on my first world tour in over a decade . . . this time traveling to Europe by sea aboard the historic Queen Mary cruise liner. By the time I got home in 2011, a major anniversary was on the horizon: twenty-five years since the release of *Paid in Full*.

THE CIPHER IS A CIRCLE

With every anniversary comes a reflection on the past, and my history with Eric B. was a significant period of my career for the fans to rally around as 2012 approached. The calls for a reunion started again in earnest, but I had no desire to look back. After almost fifteen years of searching, I was in a place where I was independent creatively, contractually, and financially. Golden Era hip-hop was riding on a wave of renewed interest. *The Seventh Seal* tour hadn't hit every city yet, the anniversary provided plenty of opportunity to perform in markets where it hadn't, and concert packages featuring "Legends of Hip-Hop" were back to selling out 10,000+ seat venues. The resurgence also meant new national endorsement campaigns, film and television scoring opportunities (and even a few small roles that weren't strictly thug), and collaborations with established and emerging artists across the world. And along the way I also became a first-time grandfather. But the twenty-fifth anniversary came and went with no reunion.

I wasn't overtly mad at Eric, and, like all family, whenever there was a life event that affected one of us, we would reach out directly or indirectly to express congratulations or concern even if years went by between those moments. There definitely was a bitter taste for doing business with him that lingered for two decades, and I think with just cause, but as the thirtieth anniversary approached, it became increasingly obvious that the audiences didn't care about all that. To be a successful artist, you must first and foremost stay true to yourself, but also realize that your fans are your affirmation and a big part of your energy. I owed it to them to at least explore the possibility of a project with Eric, and a mutual friend was trying to make that happen. "Okay, have Eric come by the crib." I wanted to get everything out in the open and move forward. With everything going on in the industry, and culture and society as a whole, I humbly thought it would be a positive moment that our fans deserved.

As soon as he walked in, I felt that old brotherly love that can only come from years of working together at a focal point of ones life. Somehow, even while he was annoying the hell out of me, he'd found a way to create a bond that transcended years of disagreement. But when I asked Eric his thoughts about the split, he told me he had nothing to apologize for.

We didn't get far in that meeting.

A few weeks later, we set up a second get together, but he again took zero responsibility for the way things had ended. By the third meeting and another series of protestations he'd done nothing wrong, I almost felt a reunion would be pointless or worse, end with such negativity we would lose even the deep down love felt for one another. Then it hit me, only I had the control to let the negativity I felt go. I didn't need to hear the words from him to make my own decisions. I called my manager Matthew Kemp, he called our original agent Cara Lewis, Cara called Live Nation, and less than five weeks later we took the stage together at the historic Apollo Theater in Harlem. More than 200 of our friends and peers—four generations of artists, activists, and icons—joined us to perform, party, and just partake in the moment, the energy and emotion igniting the sold-out crowd. That was July 7th, 2017, thirty years to the day since two teenagers from New York released one of hip-hop's most iconic albums.

■ ■ ■

Whatever your medium and whatever your level of talent or accomplishment, the first step to unleashing your creative potential is creating connection. Connect with your purpose; connect with your environment; connect with your inspirations; connect with your audience; and connect with the universal energies that encircle and encapsulate all of us. Anyone can learn tricks and techniques to perfect their craft and follow the examples of masters before them, but the connection you have to yourself must be the ultimate artistic guide. You are your benchmark to success. You are your competition. You are the manifestation of cymatic vibration that shapes the world around you.

My music has always been about trying to spread positivity and wisdom. I want to continue to spread that throughout hip-hop and beyond. I want to inspire and build people's consciousness. I want my art to elevate understanding, motivate thinking, evoke emotion, and compel action that changes the world. I want what I build to stand forever. I wasn't being a positive rapper to not have a positive effect. I wasn't trying to be a conscious rapper to not spread consciousness. I haven't saved the world, but I have taught, through my rhymes, ways for people to save themselves. For me, consciousness, spirituality, and creativity come first. Remaining true to the principles that guide my life and rhymes means staying on the path. "The alpha, with no omega."

ACKNOWLEDGMENTS

I need to begin by thanking the Creator, for without him, nothing would be possible. All praises due to Allah.

To my mother and my father, my brothers, my sisters, and my blessed and beautiful children for surrounding me with love and inspiration.

I'd like to thank the many teachers who influenced me as I grew: Miss Connors (now Page), Miss Thompkins (now Bonaparte), Miss McLane, and Mr. Kubo, my band teacher and football coach and good friend.

I've been heavily influenced by a lot of musicians I need to recognize up front. The list could go on, but John Coltrane, Michael Jackson, Stevie Wonder, Marvin Gaye, and so many others showed me what it means to create music that can reach people in a certain way. Thank you, Ruth Brown, whose lessons I hold dear to this day and to the greatest hip-hop artists that walked these streets: Grandmaster Caz, Melle Mel, Grandmaster Flash, Kool Moe Dee, Grand Wizard Theodore, Afrika Bambaataa, Kool Herc, and the Fantastic Five. A piece of all of you fills these pages. And thank you to Eric B. for starting this journey with me when we were basically kids and still performing next to me as we've become grown men.

Thank you and rest lightly, Bert Padell, my business manager of thirty years and a close friend. To Russell Simmons, Lyor Cohen, Cara Lewis, and the rest of my original executive team for being there at the start. To my longtime manager and friend Matthew Kemp—thank you for both understanding and providing what an artist like myself needs to succeed. To Tracy Sherrod, Bakari Kitwana, Matthew Guma, and the entire team at HarperCollins who brought this project together.

To Muhammad Ali, whose dedication to his craft and, even more, to his principles have proved one of the biggest influences in my life.

And to my ride or die, my wife, Felicia, for standing by me before anything and every day since.

ABOUT THE AUTHOR

Rakim reigns as one of hip-hop's most transformative artists. Along with his partner Eric B., he recorded 1987's *Paid in Full,* the landmark recording that MTV named "the greatest hip-hop album of all time." Rakim's inimitable style of lyrics, which has drawn comparisons to jazz icon Thelonious Monk, have been cited as an influence on a wide range of top-selling musicians, including Jay-Z, Nas, Eminem, Tupac, 50 Cent, and the Notorious B.I.G. Rakim is the recipient of the 2012 BET I Am Hip-Hop trophy, the 2013 BET Hip-Hop Lifetime Achievement Award, the National Black Writers Museum Lifetime Achievement Honor, and the VH1 Hip-Hop Honors. He is an inductee to the LINY Music Hall of Fame and a Rock and Roll Hall of Fame nominee. He lives with his extended family at his home in Pennsylvania.